POLICING
MULTI-ETHNIC
NEIGHBORHOODS

3/26/13

Recent Titles in
Contributions in Criminology and Penology
Series Advisor: Marvin Wolfgang

POLICING MULTI-ETHNIC NEIGHBORHOODS

The Miami Study and Findings for Law Enforcement in the United States

GEOFFREY P. ALPERT
and
ROGER G. DUNHAM

Contributions in Criminology and
Penology, Number 20

GREENWOOD PRESS

New York · Westport, Connecticut · London

Library of Congress Cataloging-in-Publication Data

Alpert, Geoffrey P.
  Policing multi-ethnic neighborhoods : the Miami study and findings
for law enforcement in the United States / Geoffrey P. Alpert and
Roger G. Dunham.
      p. cm.—(Contributions in criminology and penology, ISSN
0732-4464 ; no. 20)
    Bibliography: p.
    ISBN 0-313-26290-X (lib. bdg. : alk. paper)
    1. Police—Florida—Miami—Public opinion. 2. Law enforcement—
Florida—Miami—Public opinion. 3. Public opinion—Florida—Miami.
4. Public relations—Florida—Miami—Police. 5. Miami (Fla.)—
Ethnic relations. 6. Neighborhood—Florida—Miami. I. Dunham,
Roger G. II. Title. III. Series.
HV8148.M43A46   1988
363.2'3'09759381—dc19   88-3112

Library of Congress Catalog Card Number: 88-3112
ISBN: 0-313-26290-X
ISSN: 0732-4464

First published in 1988

Greenwood Press, Inc.
88 Post Road West, Westport, Connecticut 06881

Printed in the United States of America

The paper used in this book complies with the
Permanent Paper Standard issued by the National
Information Standards Organization (Z39.48-1984).

10 9 8 7 6 5 4 3 2 1

To Chief Dale Bowlin
and the Metro-Dade Police Department

Contents

Illustrations

FIGURES

TABLES

Preface

The impetus for this study is as much a function of the unique social environment of Miami as it is a function of the scholarly interests of the authors. Miami in the 1980s is truly a remarkable natural laboratory for the observation of social phenomena due to its rich ethnic composition and its recent Latin immigration. *The Miami Herald* reported on May 3, 1987:

"In the historical blink of an eye, Dade (county) has undergone the single most dramatic ethnic transformation of any major American city in this century," said Charles Blowers, chief of the research division of the Dade planning department.

Despite the near-doubling of the population since 1960, fewer non-Hispanic whites live in Dade now. They have declined from 80 percent of the population to 37 percent.

Eighty-four of every 100 voters who moved out of Dade in 1984 and registered elsewhere were non-Hispanic whites, according to the county elections department study (Section B, p. 1).

A combination of historical and current events has created a diversified cosmopolitan center with a distinct international composition that sits in the crossroads between North and South America. These events have created enormous social change, focused within one relatively small geographic area.

As a result of this type of social change, new challenges arise in the social order. Social agencies are faced with new and perplexing issues and problems. An important antecedent to our study is a set of serious problems which face the police in Miami and in many other urban areas. These problems challenge traditional policing in newly established and rapidly changing multi-ethnic communities. While these issues exist in most urban areas, they became evident and were highlighted in Miami by several riots which were triggered by conflict between police officers and minority suspects.

Ethnicity seemed to complicate every police procedure and every encounter between the police and the public. Police administrators searched for solutions to these problems inherent in this explosive community. Improving training, rewriting procedures, and the decentralization of administrative duties were just some of the proposed solutions. After considerable effort, it was realized that precious little information was available about members of the various ethnic groups and their views toward police and policing. More information was needed to guide these proposed solutions. How do members of each ethnic community conceptualize the police? What are their cultural expectations? Which policing techniques will receive community support and the cooperation of the law-abiding residents and which will be rejected with non-cooperation and perhaps violence? In effect, which police technique will be effective tools for the maintenance of order and the control of crime in each of the neighborhoods?

The Command Staff of the Metro-Dade Police Department was preparing to incorporate some major changes, and recognized their need for information. They asked us to conduct research into the differences among the various ethnic neighborhoods which could guide their policy decisions. Since it was thought that the genesis of the problem was the lack of understanding of the complexities involved in this dynamic, multiethnic community, a basic understanding of the cultural differences and collective attitudes about policing was necessary. Access to this information would enable police decision-makers to sort out effective ways of maintaining order, controlling crime and providing services in each area.

We introduced the neighborhood concept as a conceptual and analytical unit to the study to help clarify the issues. To aid further in directing our investigation, we introduced an inter-action model which focuses on the interaction between the in-formal system of social control within the various neighbor-hoods and the formal system of social control of the police. Theoretically, this integration of the two levels of social control provides the greatest effectiveness in controlling crime and protecting citizens. A common thread tying together the chapters of this book is the attempt to decipher differences among the various ethnic neighborhoods concerning attitudes toward police and policing. In addition, we examine policy implications based upon these differences.

The Miami study has implications for other urban areas. The results of the research are surprising and encouraging; they provide information which can be helpful to researchers, planners and police administrators. The study includes socio-historical background material, conceptual and analytical frameworks, methods, data analysis, and data interpretation chapters. The conclusions include warning signals and suggestions to police and other urban planners.

The significance of these findings revolves around the main conclusion that residence in a specific neighborhood is a more influential factor than gender or ethnicity in explaining variation in attitudes toward policing. The implications of this conclusion are that the police officer's effectiveness could be enhanced greatly if he received training specific to the district he or she patrols. This training includes knowledge concerning area-specific characteristics of the neighborhoods in the officer's district and the most appropriate and effective policing styles for citizens of those neighborhoods.

In this context, it was found that attitudes about different styles of policing do not vary among the officers assigned to the different districts. Apparently, officers do not believe it is necessary to modify their styles of policing significantly when working in different districts. This indicates that police in the different neighborhoods do not have differing styles of policing to match the unique characteristics of the neighborhoods.

Another finding which has important implications for police-community relations in general and for effective policing specifically, is that there exists an agreement among all groups that police must use discretion in following their procedures. This finding indicates considerable citizen support for individualized community policing styles. However, the use of discretion is not accepted without reservation. All of the groups, with the exception of residents in one low-income housing project, *disagreed* with the use of discretion when it is based on ethnicity.

Another important implication of this research is that the attitudes toward different levels of our social system (i.e., social institutions in general, the criminal justice system, the police) are interrelated. First, attitudes toward one level (i.e., police) may be nested in attitudes toward a more general level (i.e., the justice system). Second, attitudes toward a more general level (i.e., social institutions in general) may indicate a generally positive or generally negative orientation that provides the basis for interpreting the attitudes toward a more specific level (i.e., the police).

Our findings indicate that those who show considerable support for the police are not people who simply have positive attitudes toward all institutions in our society. Most have some special regard for the police.

The converse analysis also speaks well for the police. Most individuals with negative attitudes toward the police also hold negative attitudes toward the entire criminal justice system. Apparently, negative attitudes about the police, unlike positive attitudes, emanate from and are closely tied to one's attitudes toward the entire system of criminal justice. These negative attitudes are part of a set of attitudes which cluster around the broader legal system and perhaps include the political system. This indicates that programs which are designed to change responses to the police and which ignore this larger attitude complex are unlikely to yield impressive results.

Overall, our findings supporting the validity of the neighborhood concept as a social unit with respect to attitudes toward the police and policing also support the need to base policing strategies and practices on neighborhood characteristics. Of course, this does not hold for all neighborhoods, but it is most important for homogeneous neighborhoods which have attitudes and values divergent from the police. We introduce an interactive model to help clarify and improve the relationship between residents of diverse neighborhoods and the police.

Policy recommendations involve some degree of decentralization and can revolve around the team concept or identification and resolution of specific problems, but move beyond both. Specifically, policing with neighborhood administrative control appears to be the best of several worlds.

Our suggestion of Positive Policing has several organizational elements which must be added to the traditional components that exist in many community-oriented policing units, to become neighborhood based. First, to reduce isolation between police and the citizens, officers must be assigned for an extended period, supervised by command staff and advised by neighborhood groups. Second, neighborhood training is essential to the success of the approach. The final policy recommendation for our proposed model includes increased institutionalized monitoring and a formal reward system. This requires an ongoing system to monitor both the neighborhood and the police.

In Chapter 1 we discuss the neighborhood unit in detail, as the basis for the conceptual and analytic framework of the research. In Chapter 2, the socio-historical context of relations between the police and the public in Dade County, Florida, is explored.

In the third chapter, we describe the methods of data collection used in this study, and explain the selection procedures for the five neighborhood samples, the police sample and the student sample. The demographic characteristics of each of the samples are summarized and the variables and measures used in the study are documented.

In Chapter 4 we give a detailed description of the findings relating to police task evaluations. The focus of this chapter is the differences in perception between the police and the public, of the various police tasks and duties.

Chapter 5 outlines the major findings on the several scales measuring attitudes toward police demeanor, the public's responsibility for controlling crime, police use of discretion in applying the law, the appropriateness of treating ethnic groups differently, and toward active patrol strategies. The focus is on neighborhood profiles and their congruence with police attitudes.

In Chapter 6 we examine the attitudes discussed in Chapter 5 within the context of more general attitude domains. The focus of this chapter is on the relationship between attitudes toward the police and attitudes toward major institutions in our society.

In the seventh and eighth chapters we discuss the conclusions based on the findings, including those concerning police task evaluations, attitudes toward the police and attitudes in the context of the more general attitude domain. In the last chapter we outline the major policy implications of this research.

We are grateful for the assistance and support of the many officers of the Metro-Dade Police Department who so willingly cooperated with our research. A special thanks goes to our families for their patience and support throughout the duration of this project. In addition, we acknowledge the work of our research assistants, Christina Pozo and Daniel "Sackman" Stubbs, and our illustrator, Jason Dunham.

POLICING
MULTI-ETHNIC
NEIGHBORHOODS

1

Introduction

The history of the police is a history of ideas. It was Sir Robert Peel, among others, whose ideas when put into practice produced what we know as the police. To gain a complete understanding of police, it has been suggested that we consider the police as an "omnibus service agency" (Clark and Sykes, 1974: 462), consider the roles of police to include those of philosopher, guide and friend (Cumming et al., 1965), and examine the activities of the police as those of keepers of the peace (Bittner, 1967). We will explore some of the extra-legal influences on police behavior with our attention focused upon the public's perception of police and police practices, and in turn, the perception of the public by the police. Our concern is with the effects of neighborhood characteristics on these perceptions. We belive these perceptions can help guide the growth and change within police organizations and influence relations between the police and the communities they serve.

NEIGHBORHOODS: A CONCEPTUAL FRAMEWORK

One of the first and most important research-related decisions concerning this study was which unit of analysis to use as the main focus. Our research could have been based upon samples from large sections of the county, total communities or more restricted neighborhoods. Our goal was to look at populations that theoretically hold different attitudes toward the police and policing, and which are easily identifiable. Based upon previous research and discussions with police administrators concerned with the development of police strategies, we were directed to the neighborhood as the most important unit of study. Considering the various structures of human organization, police officials were the most perplexed by these residential areas and the problems related to the development of strategies for policing them. The kinds of citizens and the quality of life that is shared within these neighborhoods, and the apparent differences among these social units raise serious questions about the need for different strategies of policing.

Neighborhoods

The neighborhood is frequently described as though it were a continuation of small-town America, a place where a true community spirit exists. When police focus on these smaller units, it allows them the opportunity to move closer to the people, and to respond more fully to their unique needs. A decentralization of police administration and an increased awareness of neighborhood differences should turn the focus of policing to meet the needs of those who share a common fate and a common style of life. It can be argued that the smaller geographical area is critical for many other social processes as well. It can generate strong neighborly relationships, mutual aid through voluntary organizations and other support networks, as opposed to the unconnected segments characteristic of so much of society. The neighborhood unit has intrinsic value because it is a concentration of people with similar backgrounds, ethnicity, lifestyle and social status.

We chose not to use the concept of community because it has been used by sociologists and others with so many different shades of meaning that it is difficult to understand and discuss with any degree of precision. Poplin (1979:4) has reviewed the many uses of the concept of community and concluded that they do not include enough in common to compare as like units of a social organization. For example, he comments on the disparity among a minority group, a large city, and a complex military organization, all referred to by social scientists as communities. We chose to use the term "neighborhood" and to apply to it some degree of conceptual rigor.

The study of neighborhoods has preoccupied sociologists since the turn of the century (see Olson, 1982). Although there were several other studies of a more empirical nature, Cooley (1909) conceptualized the neighborhood as one of the three principal forms of social organization exemplifying the "primary group" (other than the family and children's play groups). Another principal intellectual influence on the study of the social aspects of neighborhoods was Robert E. Park, who wrote:

In the course of time every section and quarter of the city takes on something of the character and qualities of its inhabitants. Each separate part of the city is inevitably stained with the peculiar sentiments of its population. The effect of this is to convert what was at first a mere geographical expression into a neighborhood, that is to say, a locality with sentiments, traditions, and a history of its own. . . . Proximity and neighborly contact are the basis of the simplest and most elementary form of association with which we have to do in the organization of city life. . . . In the social and political organization of the city it is the smallest local unit (1915:579–580).

Park's conceptualization of the neighborhood inspired a research agenda that continued for two decades.

The prestigious American Public Health Association adopted the neighborhood concept in the late 1940s as a "healthful and hygienic" standard for planning, designing, and managing the residential environment (Banerjee and Baer, 1984:2). Subsequently, planners all over the world have adopted its purpose of creating a sense of community, promoting and protecting the public health, safety and welfare. "For more than fifty years, it has been virtually the sole basis for formally organizing residential space" (Banerjee and Baer, 1984:2).

Beginning in the 1950s, the neighborhood concept has come under strong attack. However, despite extraordinary social change in the society and the numerous criticisms claiming the obsolescence of the neighborhood concept, the local community persists. The neighborhood as a social form has changed, but it is an adaptive mechanism which remains an important source of the individual's integration into the larger society.

Critics of the neighborhood concept have claimed that the role of the residential community has weakened (Keller, 1968; Stein, 1960; Webber, 1970). They argued that the neighborhood is no longer important to the identity and sense of belonging of its inhabitants, and that local units of population are no longer able to establish and maintain a stable moral order. It has been claimed that the neighborhood is "an increasingly obsolete contrivance geared to the needs of yesterday's rural migrant in need of a sheltered village-like existence, even though the city-dweller has become increasingly urbane, using a nonplace urban realm as a satisfying environment" (Banerjee and Baer, 1984:5–6). City life, with increased means of mobility and increasing social complexity, has destroyed the small residential community as a social primary group. Today, city dwellers are more likely to develop primary associations based on similar interests including religion, profession, age and children, rather than on ecological proximity. It is argued that changes in transportation and communication have increased the possibilities of human contact over greater distances and have produced a "community without propinquity" (Webber, 1970).

A major alternative theory has emerged to conceptualize neighborhoods which is called the "community of limited liability model." Janowitz (1967) and Greer (1962), among others, have argued this view of urban dwellers, depicting them as having only a contingent commitment to their local areas. According to this model, residents of cities can satisfy their need for interpersonal relationships over a large territory. It is only the residents with the greatest economic and social stake in the local area (i.e., childrearing households and property owners) who have a strong and sustained attachment to the local area. Therefore, according to this model, commitment to the neighborhood is voluntary and partial, and competes with other social units.

One commentator (Olson, 1982:505) asks whether neighborhoods are becoming impersonal arenas devoid of intimate social life and whether they still function as local communities.

Research and conventional wisdom tell us it is true that peoples' lives are more complex than previously thought, and that neighborhoods have undergone considerable change in the past fifty years. However, there has persisted, for many, a sense of local sentiment, close-knit networks, and a stable moral order, especially in working-class, culturally homogeneous neighborhoods (Greenberg and Rohe, 1986).

We seem to have entered yet another stage in metropolitan growth: the beginning of revitalization of the central city, that is, the renewal of neighborhoods and the housing stock, prompted by a slowing of the exodus to the suburbs, the choice of many young, childless couples and singles to remain in the central city, and the movement back to the city of suburbanites whose children are grown. Together, these and other factors have prompted a renewed interest in the urban neighborhood, especially as the smallest unit within which to mount a social and physical renewal of the central city (Olson, 1982:492–493).

The 1970s witnessed a tide of social activism at the neighborhood level, and federal urban policy became linked to the concept of community at the neighborhood level. David Morris and Karl Hess' book, *Neighborhood Power: The New Localism* (1975), represents a part of this social activism. They argue that neighborhood units deserve increased attention, not simply because they are practical, but because they may be necessary. It is argued that today's "boasted economies of scale in our large cities are hardly even to be taken seriously after a common sense look around us" (Morris and Hess, 1975:4). They point out the problems of scale in the police departments, trash collection, fire departments and most of all, big city politics. For example:

Police departments, huge and depersonalized, are far removed from the days of the policeman who was our protector, friend, and neighbor. One result has been a wave of scandals which continues to rock major cities. The other is the sense that big-city police forces are simply incapable of dealing with ordinary street crime—that only action at the neighborhood level can do the job (Morris and Hess, 1975:4).

Overall, the history of research and theory on the neighborhood unit suggests clearly that the metropolis is characterized by a continued, but a somewhat selective, pattern of localized activity. The results from a number of ethnographic studies of working-class urban neighborhoods in the 1960s has demonstrated the persistence of local sentiment, close-knit networks, and a stable moral order in culturally homogeneous neighborhoods (Fried and Gleicher, 1961; Gans, 1962; Suttles, 1972). To answer his own question posed earlier, Olson concluded:

The old question, "What is meant by neighborhood?" is replaced with "What kind of neighborhood is this?" . . . The most chronic problem—the debate over whether the urban neighborhood is disappearing—has now virtually been resolved. Once the conceptualization of the local community expanded to account for types of neighborhoods, it became possible to identify certain residential areas as nonneighborhoods without suggesting the decline of the urban local community (1982:508).

A more constructive avenue for neighborhood research is to examine how and under what conditions the local community is related to social integration at the different levels of society.

Our use of the neighborhood concept focuses on the social unit, rather than on the ecological unit. This distinction between ecological factors and dimensions of social organization is important in clarifying the difference between the urban community and the urban neighborhood. "Whereas the urban community represents ecological considerations of human life, particularly the social space involved in the daily transactions of sustenance, the urban neighborhood represents the patterns of social organization (located in residential areas) focused on day-to-day activities" (Olson, 1982:495). Our definition is that presented by Park and Burgess (1925) to categorize sections of the city they called "natural areas." Natural areas are *sections of the city where residents share common lifestyles, are of the same cultural types, and have identifiable boundaries* (cited in Olson, 1982:496). A further aspect of the neighborhood, as defined here, is that it remains a social group. The residents communicate with each other about local issues on a regular basis and feel some sense of identification and attachment to the area and its people.

It should not, however, be assumed that all neighborhoods have shared norms for appropriate public behavior. A number of studies have found that these shared norms are less likely to develop in low-income neighborhoods that are heterogeneous with regard to ethnic composition, family type, or lifestyle than they are in low-income, culturally homogeneous neighborhoods or in middle-class neighborhoods (Greenberg and Rohe, 1986:85).

However, the definition used here incorporates the idea that residents of different neighborhoods are marked by a particular pattern of life, and perhaps even a subculture of their own with social traditions. At the very least, within its physical and symbolic boundaries, a neighborhood contains inhabitants having something in common. Even if this commonality is only the current sharing of an environment, it gives the residents a certain collective character and alternatives for adapting to the larger society (Keller, 1968:90). The importance of the neighborhood as a unit of analysis lies in its dual characteristic of combining both ecological and interpersonal aspects of human interaction (Caplow and Forman, 1950:357).

ANALYTIC FRAMEWORK: AN INTERACTIVE MODEL

The neighborhood is a major source of social integration in the large-scale society. It has persisted despite tremendous growth in cities through urbanization, through substantial decline, suburbanization and disaffection with city life. It has done so, in large part, because it provides a valuable source of integration within a large, complex and diverse culture. These "natural areas" as they were referred to by Park and Burgess (1925) provide ways that residents can identify alternative means of relating to the larger, complex society. "Neighborhood differentiation is the adaptive mechanism which leads to these alternative responses and thus helps explain the residents' integration into the larger society" (Olson, 1982:493).

The Neighborhood and Social Integration

A question of importance to our analytical framework is how and under what conditions the neighborhood is related to integration at the societal level. Janowitz and Suttles (1978) discuss a generalized model for examining this issue by which the neighborhood unit is proposed as the basis for both self-regulation or social control and as the platform for political participation in the general society. "Properly perceived, the local community is a staging area in which diverse interests are mobilized and joined in an aggregative political process that can shape, and strengthen, and legitimize the actions of political and administrative hierarchies" (Janowitz and Suttles, 1978:105). The neighborhood is conceptualized as part of a three-level model containing the social bloc at the first level, the organizational community at the second and the aggregated metropolitan community at the final level. Each level of response forms a part of the response at the next level. Thus, local issues are aggregated at one level until they find a response at the next. The local neighborhood level, then, has the function of creating and making available to its residents ways of interacting with and adapting to the higher levels of the social structure. When successful, "local values become articulated with the larger policies and practices of the society" (Olson, 1982:509). This process achieves some level of social integration, which Olson (1978) calls vertical integration. Horizontal integration occurs within the local community when the residents coalesce on common issues.

Those consensual concerns—together with such identified factors as length of residence, neighboring, established boundaries, and social networks—contribute to social control and cohesion at the local level and become the "staging area" for being joined in the aggregative political process (Olson, 1982:510).

Poplin (1979:6) lists some of the characteristics of what he calls "moral communities" (as opposed to mass societies). A brief description of these selected characteristics can give us a better idea of what neighborhood characteristics contribute to our sense of integration into the larger society.

1. *Identification*: members of the neighborhood have a sense of belonging to a significant, meaningful group. This is opposed to members

of mass societies who have a sense of being "cut off" from meaningful group association or feel alienated.

2. *Moral Unity*: members of the neighborhood have a sense of pursuing common goals and feel a oneness with other neighborhood members. This is opposed to moral fragmentation that is experienced by members of mass societies because they pursue divergent goals and feel no sense of oneness with other members of the society.

3. *Involvement*: members of the neighborhood are submerged in various groups and fulfill a need to participate in these groups. This is opposed to a feeling of disengagement experienced by members of mass societies because they have no meaningful group membership and feel no need to participate in the collective activities of various groups.

4. *Wholeness*: members of the neighborhood regard each other as whole persons who are of intrinsic significance and worth, as opposed to a sense of segmentation caused by members of the mass society regarding each other as simply a means to an end, and thereby assign no intrinsic worth or significance to the individual.

Neighborhoods will differ in the type of characteristics shared by their members as well as the level of intensity to which these residents adhere to the characteristics. Some neighborhoods will include members who share many common goals and values, while others will have members share relatively few characteristics. There is no set rule for what constitutes a common goal, as often commonalities change and the intensity to which one believes in them fluctuate. What is important is the sense of security one has with his or her neighbors.

Nisbet (1960) points out a consequence of a decreasing sense of meaning and security in an increasingly complex society. He notes that our society can provide us with the miracles of mass production, mass education, mass communication and mass government, but it cannot provide us with a sense of belonging, security, and meaning.

The state does not even serve the security need. No large scale organization can really meet the psychic demand of individuals because, by its very nature, it is too large, too complex, too bureaucratized, and altogether too aloof from the residual meanings which human beings

live by. The state can enlist popular enthusiasm, can conduct cru-
sades, can mobilize on behalf of great causes, such as war, but as a
regular and normal means of meeting human needs for recognition,
fellowship, security, and membership, it is inadequate (Nisbet, 1960:82).

Integration at the neighborhood level, then, can be defined
as *those tendencies within the small and relatively homogeneous residential area that give its residents a common orientation, a sense of
belonging and participation* that they find absent in the larger society. This sense of integration at the neighborhood level makes
them feel a part of the larger society by providing them with
ways of adapting to and interfacing with the larger system. In
sum, a cohesive neighborhood structure provides a way for
residents to identify with and relate to the larger society, and
therefore is a component of social integration.

The Neighborhood and Social Control

Cohesive neighborhoods, being one of Cooley's basic primary groups, are an important source of informal social control. Park (1925:23) contrasts the potential for social control between face-to-face primary relations (such as found in cohesive
neighborhoods) and indirect or secondary relations characteristic of larger urban areas.

The interactions which take place among the members of a community so constituted [such as a cohesive neighborhood] are immediate
and unreflecting. Intercourse is carried on largely within the region of
instinct and feeling. Social control arises, for the most part sponta-
neously, in direct response to personal influences and public sentiment. It is the result of a personal accommodation, rather than the
formulation of a rational and abstract principle (Park, 1925:23).

When these intimate relationships of the primary groups are
weakened, social control is gradually dissolved. The resulting
indirect or secondary relationships have a much different effect
on social control.

It is characteristic of city life [in the absence of neighborhood cohesion] that all sorts of people meet and mingle together who never fully comprehend one another. The anarchist and the club man, the priest and the Levite, the actor and the missionary who touch elbows on the street still live in totally different worlds. So complete is the segregation of vocational classes that it is possible within the limits of the city to live in an isolation almost as complete as that of some remote rural community (Park, 1925:26).

Park observed differences between social control based upon mores and neighborhood cohesion, and social control based upon indirect and secondary relationships and positive law. The latter is much weaker and less capable of establishing order.

More recently, Greenberg and Rohe (1986:79) have reviewed the empirical research on the relationship between informal control and crime. They concluded that emotional attachment to the neighborhood, perceived responsibility for the control over the neighborhood, and the expectation that oneself or one's neighbors would intervene in a criminal event, are associated with low crime rates. This evidence suggests a relationship between the informal control of a cohesive neighborhood and crime. They suggest that more research should be conducted on the process by which norms for public behavior develop in neighborhoods and are communicated to residents.

Informal social control in the residential context refers to the development, observance, and enforcement of local norms for appropriate public behavior (Greenberg and Rohe, 1986:80). It is the process by which individual behavior is influenced by a group, and usually functions to maintain a minimum level of predictability in the behavior of group members, and to promote the well-being of the group as a whole.

Formal social control is based on written rules or laws and prescribed punishments for violating these rules and laws. The police and the courts are the institutions most directly charged with maintaining order under formal social controls. The means of formal social control are not very effective without the direct support of the informal means of control. The combination and the interaction of the two is central to the analytical framework of this research.

THE INTEGRATION OF FORMAL AND
INFORMAL SOCIAL CONTROLS

Informal social control is not based upon written rules and laws, but relies upon local norms and traditions. The effectiveness of the formal system of control depends upon citizens who initiate the enforcement of these norms and laws. The formal means of control, then, becomes a backup or support of local enforcement. The informal sanctions applied to violators are often subtle, yet powerful, such as a raised eyebrow or gossip. Other times they are more forceful, such as the withdrawal of approval, exclusion from the group, warnings or threats. In more extreme cases, the informal system may invoke the formal system. But still, much of the power of the formal control measures remain with the local group. The stigma of a police car in one's driveway, being handcuffed and placed in a police car in front of family members and long-time friends and neighbors, and the sting of the gossip is feared much more in cohesive neighborhoods than the actual punishments of the formal system. Of course, maximum effectiveness of the control system requires that the norms and values of the informal system be consistent with those of the formal system. Wilson and Kelling advocate this level of integration:

The essence of the police role in maintaining order is to reinforce the informal control mechanisms of the community itself. The police cannot, without committing extraordinary resources, provide a substitute for that informal control. On the other hand, to reinforce those natural forces the police must accommodate them (1982:34).

If the local values and customs of a neighborhood view the police as outsiders and the arrest situation as the imposition of unfair and biased rules upon fellow residents, then stigma of the arrest situation is absent and the informal control system works against the formal system.

The behavior of those outside the group may also be influenced by informal social control. Neighborhood residents may individually or collectively exert pressure on those outside the group to conform to group-defined norms for appropriate public behavior. The rewards and punishments may differ from those used to influence the behavior of insiders, but nonetheless can be effective. Control may take the form of close surveillance or questioning, or verbal correction of behavior seen as inappropriate in the local context (Greenberg and Rohe, 1986).

Our earlier discussion concluded that informal social control is not present in every neighborhood; rather it is a variable that differs both in form and degree among neighborhoods. In other words, not all neighborhoods have a substantial degree of cohesion with regard to norms and values specifying appropriate public behavior. Many lack any degree of fundamental integration, and thereby the means for an effective informal social control system (see Greenberg and Rohe, 1986:81).

More specifically, the results of research on neighborhoods indicate that shared norms are less likely to develop in low-income neighborhoods that are heterogeneous with regard to ethnic composition, family type, or lifestyle, than they are in low-income, culturally homogeneous neighborhoods or in middle-class neighborhoods (see Greenberg and Rohe, 1986; Merry, 1981). Residents of low-income heterogeneous neighborhoods tend to be more suspicious of each other, to perceive less commonality with other residents, and tend to feel less control over their neighborhood than do the residents of more homogeneous neighborhoods.

Low-income neighborhoods which develop strong informal control tend to be characterized by the dominance of one group. As Merry emphasizes, "the social order in a neighborhood depends on the presence of a dominant group that perceives itself as responsible for public order" (1981:230–231). When this influence is absent in low-income neighborhoods, distrust and hostility tend to prevail, leaving only the formal means of social control (police and courts) to control crime and maintain order.

For example, many inner-city black neighborhoods lack this dominant cultural group. Even though the residents are all black, housing discrimination and other factors result in neighborhoods which vary considerably in the social values, lifestyle and family type characteristic of its residents (Erbe, 1975). As a result of this diversity, residents have little consensus on conceptions of appropriate public behavior, and informal social control within the neighborhood tends to be weak. In extreme cases, the conceptions of appropriate public behavior are in conflict among neighborhood residents.

The situation in predominately white, middle-class neighborhoods is much different. These neighborhoods tend to be more homogeneous due to self-selection resulting from the greater freedom of choice in locating a residence. Residents tend to self-select their location based upon similarities of other residents to their family type, lifestyle and values. This process tends to group residents according to their basic underlying assumptions of appropriate public behavior and values. Therefore, informal social control tends to be much more developed in these types of neighborhoods, when compared to low-income neighborhoods.

It is this and other types of neighborhood differentiation that require an interactive model for effective policing. A knowledge of neighborhood differences must be developed, and police must respond to those different characteristics in controlling crime and protecting residents. A failure to do this often results in the formal system of social control attempting to operate alone or even in opposition to the more powerful informal system of control.

An Interactive Model

We have already established that the neighborhood unit remains a social unit as well as an ecological concept, even though the neighborhood unit has undergone considerable change. These changes have resulted in considerable variation among neighborhoods in their degree of cohesiveness, and the strength of their informal social control systems. However, we have established that neighborhood context can provide an important source of integration into the larger society for its residents. In fact, cohesive neighborhoods provide alternative means for residents to respond to and adapt to the larger, more complex society. Finally, cohesive neighborhoods incorporate an important system of informal social control that can be crucial to establishing order and controlling crime, if it is integrated into the formal social control system involving the police and the courts. The key is the interaction between the formal social control system of the larger community, and the informal control systems operating in the various neighborhoods.

One of the early functions of developing urban police forces was to establish social regulation to supplement their law-enforcement duties. This need was created as police effectiveness declined, as urbanization increased, and as communities became more cosmopolitan (Black, 1980; Kelling, 1985). In the most disorderly parts of American cities, the traditional police officer became an "institution" who responded to a "moral mandate" for informal social control in situations where individuals violated community or neighborhood norms and impinged on the personal and property rights of others. This role, often referred to as the "street justice" function (see Sykes, 1986), refers to police behavior that is responsive to situational and organizational factors which reflect the interpretations of community needs and expectations by the police. "Street justice," then, is a response to a community or neighborhood mandate that something be done about situations where formal institutions cannot or will not respond for a variety of reasons (Sykes, 1986).

What was once a major function of the newly established urban police force later became a subject of widespread concern and criticism of the police. Originally, the "street justice" function was a way of responding to local differences in norms and citizens' mandates for the police. When this function became linked to ethnic and racial prejudice in the 1950s and 1960s, however, it became a target for decades of reform (Sykes, 1986).

"Street Justice" appeared to be an anomaly and was targeted for reform on many fronts, most effectively by the "professional paradigm" which emphasized the enforcement role of the police. . . . In recent years, a challenge to the liberal reformers emerged which questioned the efficacy of these reforms. This challenge can be referred to as the "order maintenance paradigm" which alleges that many discretionary police activities cannot be reduced to bureaucratic due process without a costly trade-off in crime control effectiveness (Sykes, 1986:498).

Samuel Walker (1984), among others, has challenged the recent "order maintenance paradigm" by asserting that it has mistakenly based its view of traditional police roles on a highly romanticized view of nineteenth-century neighborhood life. Walker assumes the decline of local community and neighborhood cohesion discussed earlier. Our analysis revealed a more recent recognition that the neighborhood concept is reasonable for many types of neighborhoods, and that the fears of a wholesale decline of the neighborhood social community were unfounded.

The traditional model of policing, whether it is labelled "street justice" or "order maintenance," represents a model of policing that integrates the informal control system of the local community with the formal control system of the police. The more recent model of policing, whether it is called "law enforcement" or "professional," attempts policing with minimal integration between the formal control system of the police and the informal control system of the local neighborhood.

The interactive model calls for policing strategies that integrate formal procedures and practices with the informal social control system operating within the various neighborhoods. To reach maximum effectiveness, police discretion and strategies must be organized within the established norms of public behavior in the cohesive neighborhood. Policies must be developed with an understanding that the neighborhood has established alternative ways which residents adapt to and cope with the larger social system, including the police, and the laws they enforce. Policy-makers need to be aware of these coping mechanisms, so that policies and procedures will reflect a harmony with them, rather than conflict. Indeed, police departments, through their policies and support structures, shape officers' attitudes and policing styles used in different communities (see Steinman, 1986).

Before this level of integration can exist, we need a better understanding of neighborhood characteristics, and the infrastructure of the informal social control. A very basic yet crucial question to be answered concerns the justification for neighborhood policing strategies. Are there significant differences among neighborhoods in the views of residents toward the police and police strategies? Peter Manning (1984) has included this question in his list of the ten major assumptions underly-

Figure 1-1.
Research on Neighborhood Context

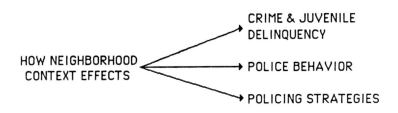

ing community policing. The community policing model assumes that there is a single or dominant public or public mood in the local area. The purpose of this research is to initiate an empirical exploration into neighborhood differences concerning views toward the police and police strategies, and to determine if and when differences are significant enough to justify a neighborhood approach to police strategies.

Neighborhood context has been studied in several ways with respect to the crime problem and policing. Each research literature points to the importance of the neighborhood context as a major factor in understanding the crime problem and police control as identified in Figure 1-1. In our next section, we turn to a discussion of the effects of neighborhood context, on crime and juvenile delinquency in general, on police behavior, and finally on the focus of our research, policing strategies. A short introduction will be followed by a brief review of the relevant research literature for each of these subject areas.

The effect of neighborhood context on crime and juvenile delinquency has been of interest to researchers for many years. As a result, there is a rich and plentiful literature addressing this important issue (Simcha-Fagan and Schwartz, 1986). Although not central to our analytical framework, this relationship emphasizes that the neighborhood contextual factors are important to this related aspect of the overall crime problem: the production of crime and juvenile delinquency. The effect of neighborhood factors on police behavior has also been of interest to police researchers. A great deal of this interest concerns the issue of neighborhood stigma and the police response to residents in a discriminatory manner consistent with the specific neighborhood identity. As with the effect on crime and delinquency, neighborhood effect on police behavior is not central to our analytical framework. It is more involved with individual police responses, rather than with the development of general police strategies which are reflective of the contextual differences of neighborhoods. The purpose of our investigation is to determine if there exist sufficient neighborhood differences in views toward policing to warrant a decentralized approach to crime control. The focus here is on developing an empirical basis for tailoring police strategies specifically to certain types of cohesive neighborhoods. A brief examination of the research literatures for each of these issues follow.

NEIGHBORHOOD CONTEXT, CRIME AND DELINQUENCY

Research examining the link between neighborhood characteristics and crime really began with the Chicago Area Project (see Shaw and McKay, 1942). The conceptual framework came directly from the work of Park and Burgess discussed earlier. A majority of the research centered around the proposition that the growth patterns of American cities tend to create characteristic types of areas that differ widely from one another. Furthermore, the location of the areas which are subject to the most rapid change, and the direction of the change in these areas are assumed to be predictable. The rapid turnover of residents in certain areas as well as aging and deterioration of the areas are viewed as basic elements in the disruption of social life. With the disruption of the social order comes high rates of crime and delinquency.

In his introduction to the first edition of the book, *Juvenile Delinquency and Urban Areas*, Ernest W. Burgess concluded:

We must realize that the brightest hope in reformation is in changing the neighborhood and in control of the gang in which the boy moves, lives, and has his being and to which he returns after his institutional treatment. And, finally, we must reaffirm our faith in prevention, which is so much easier, cheaper, and more effective than cure and which begins with the home, the play group, the local school, the church, and the neighborhood (Shaw and McKay, 1942:xiii).

James F. Short, Jr., in the introduction to the revised edition (1969:xxvi), identified it as one of the few projects to have a lasting impact on social science. Short concluded that since the original publication of the findings, little has happened to alter the factual picture presented, and that theoretical advances and more recent programs of delinquency control are in large part extensions or modifications of those suggested by Shaw and McKay (1969:xxvi). This massive documentation of empirical regularities, as found in Shaw and McKay's work, and that of their associates, is indeed rare in the social sciences.

The majority of the empirical research conducted since Shaw and McKay's original work has been devoted to aggregate-level analysis and to examining and elaborating their propositions. Included are analyses of the relationships between aspects or characteristics of ecologically defined areas and their rates of juvenile or adult criminality (i.e., Lander, 1954; Bordua, 1958; Chilton, 1964; Polk, 1957). In an interesting study by Clark and Wenninger (1962) the researchers attempted to resolve some apparent conflicts in the literature concerning the relationship between socioeconomic class and illegal behavior. These findings led to the conclusion that it was the "status area" or "neighborhood climate" that determined the level of delinquency. The predominant social class of the area set the tone of the neighborhood climate, but middle-class boys in a predominantly lower-class area had delinquency rates characteristic of lower-class boys. Further, the lower-class boys in a predominantly middle-class area had delinquency rates characteristic of middle-class boys. Neighborhood climate was the most important variable explaining rates of delinquency, which demonstrated the "great power of prevailing norms within a status area" (Clark and Wenninger, 1962:225).

Some of the recent studies have introduced additional aggregate level concepts hypothesized as structural effects which have supported the general relationship between neighborhood context and crime (i.e., Hagan, Gillis and Chan, 1978; Sampson, 1985; Bursik and Webb, 1982; Messner, 1982; Cohen and Land, 1984; Simcha-Fagan and Schwartz, 1986).

The relevance of this literature to the present study is that it demonstrates that contextual variables are found to be important for understanding criminal behavior and delinquency. The one consistent finding throughout this literature is that neighborhood is an important variable and must be considered when examining issues related to crime and delinquency. For example, in one of the most recent studies, and one with the strongest methodology, the researchers factored in both individual-level characteristics and community-level characteristics (Simcha-Fagan and Schwartz, 1986). They found that community-level effects are significant after controlling for individual-level characteristics, and that the community effects on delinquency are to a large extent mediated by socialization experiences. An operational definition of crime depends upon the mutual ways police adapt to local circumstances, and to the ways community members interact with the police. Thus, this literature provides added evidence for our analytical framework which focuses upon the interaction between the informal control system of the neighborhood and the formal control system, including the police and the courts.

Neighborhood Context and Police Behavior

Michael Banton observed in his study of British and American police departments that police provided different services in different neighborhoods (1964:181). He speculated that the police are more likely to adopt a service perspective in a neighborhood similar to their own. The less social distance between the officer and the citizens in the neighborhood, the more likely the officer will adopt a helping orientation to encounters with citizens. Banton found that as the social distance between citizens of the neighborhood and the attending officer increased, the officer was more likely either to respond more formally and officially to citizens, or to be reluctant to become involved at all.

David Bordua (1958) argues that police practices vary considerably from one neighborhood context to the next, and notes that this type of particularistic police response is a necessary adaptive component of the police role. Rumbaut and Bittner (1979) point out that it was the study of this type of police discretion which led scholars to regard the law as only one factor influencing police behavior. This discovery turned the attention of scholars to the study of some of the many other factors which could influence police behavior.

Police research in the 1960s and 1970s helped develop the theme that to understand police behavior, one must consider the neighborhood context in which the police operate. Werthman and Piliavin (1967), for example, found that police behavior is motivated, in part, by a set of expectations regarding what is considered appropriate conduct in a particular neighborhood. They report that police divide the population and the geographical territory in their jurisdiction into readily understandable categories, and conclude that "residence in a *neighborhood* is the most general indicator used by police to select a sample of potential law violators" (1967:76).

Recently, there has been a continued interest in how the police respond in different neighborhood contexts (Sherman, 1986; Smith, 1986; Skolnick and Bayley, 1986; Taub et al., 1984; Decker, 1981). The primary focus of this research has been to assess the degree to which discretionary police behavior, such as making arrests, filing reports of crimes, and exercising coercive authority toward citizens are influenced by the type of neighborhood in which the encounters between the police and citizens occur. Douglas Smith (1986), from data involving 5,688 police-citizen contacts observed in three metropolitan areas, observed that police act differently in different neighborhood contexts. He concludes that theories of police discretion must explicitly recognize the contextual variability of police decision making (Smith, 1986:339). He has identified two specific questions addressed throughout this research literature (1986:314). These include: (1) To what extent do characteristics of neighborhoods directly influence police behavior after controlling for the influence of encounter-specific or situational factors on police behavior; and (2) To what degree do police respond differently to cues in encounters in different types of neighborhoods. Each of these questions concerns the degree to which police actions are influenced by the neighborhood context in which the encounters with citizens occur.

In response to these questions, a substantial portion of this research has focused on how the police categorize the "good" and "bad" areas or neighborhoods, and discriminate against citizens in the "bad" areas. This process has been called ecological contamination (see Smith, 1986). In other words, the police react as if everyone in the "bad" areas is suspect, and treat them harshly, as though they possess the moral liability of the particular area.

The relevance of this research to the present study is that it demonstrates that neighborhood context is at least a crucial variable for understanding police behavior and police discretion. Although our interest is more directed to general police strategies than the particularistic responses of individual police officers, this literature provides evidence for the importance of neighborhood context in the more general interactive framework involving crime, police behavior and police strategies.

Neighborhood Context and Police Strategies

Lawrence Sherman (1986:347) argues that there is considerable variation among neighborhoods in the ways the police manage resources, exercise discretion, and decide when to respond to problems. Yet, he concludes, there is little relativity in basic police strategy. Because of this, he argues for a mixed-strategy model to policing particular communities based upon their unique characteristics. Unfortunately, there is little empirical data assessing the assumption that residents of neighborhoods or communities have distinct preferences or dislikes for specific police strategies or practices. Indeed, it is unclear whether these preferences or dislikes vary from one type of neighborhood to another.

William Foote Whyte made some relevant observations more than forty years ago in *Street Corner Society* (1943). He found sharply contrasting social pressures that existed in different neighborhoods and concluded they were important consequences of urban life. He noted that the police must adapt to these sharply conflicting social pressures, and observed that an almost universal adaptation by police was the development of different standards of correct or acceptable conduct in different neighborhoods. Thus, what might be tolerated by police in one neighborhood would quickly be acted against in another. Whyte noted more specifically that the police must adapt to these different standards of correct or acceptable conduct prevalent in the different neighborhoods.

There are prevalent in society two general conceptions of the duties of the police officer. Middle-class people feel that he should enforce the law without fear or favor. Cornerville people and many of the officers themselves believe that the policeman should have the confidence of the people in his area so that he can settle many difficulties in a personal manner without making arrests. These two conceptions are in a large measure contradictory. (Whyte, 1943:136)

Whyte's observations have been echoed by many, but tested by few. Other researchers have continued this theme in the context of community policing, arguing that effective policing requires an understanding of different citizen expectations and values toward police practices.

It is apparent that neighborhood differences are important to effective policing, and that the police routinely operate differently in some specific ways in response to neighborhood differences. However, it is not clear to what degree departmental strategies differ with respect to neighborhood differences. It is unfortunate that there is insufficient data to direct appropriately these responses. The focus of our research is on how residents of different neighborhoods evaluate specific police practices, an important data base for decision-making concerning specific strategies for specific neighborhoods. Several studies are directly relevant to our research in that they examine specific neighborhood differences in attitudes toward the police and policing.

Two important studies deserve our attention. First, Schuman and Gruenberg (1972:386) concluded that the primary factor explaining satisfaction and dissatisfaction with police services is neighborhood. They found race to be an important factor as well, but the within-race variation was largely accounted for by neighborhood. Apparently, the interaction of race and neighborhood accounts for much of the variation in attitudes toward the police and police services. Second, Walker, et al. (1972) also found neighborhood context to be an important factor in attitudes toward the police and more specifically in the amount of support residents give to the police. The general finding from this research indicates that involuntary contacts with the police contributed to the more negative attitudes exhibited by blacks than by others toward the police. However, they found that it was the nature of the contact and the cumulative contextual effect within the neighborhood that best accounted for the low level of support for the police shown among blacks.

Our study goes beyond these research findings to examine more directly attitude differences in five culturally distinct neighborhoods. Research on attitudes toward police practices typically uses samples combining various and diverse social groups to represent large populations. While this approach can be used to characterize whole geographical areas, it may mask the unique attitudes of the various social groups (Sullivan, Dunham and Alpert, 1987; Scaglion and Condon, 1980). In turn, findings resulting from attempts to characterize generalized attitudes of an entire population are of limited use to police planners and trainers, since the police must respond to the needs and concerns of citizens that are often unique to their cultural groups. Given the mixed social character of our cities and the mosaic that makes our social fabric, police administrators must decide how to prepare officers to function effectively in the many diverse cultural environments they serve. For this and other reasons, there has been a significant resurgence of interest in community-specific policing.

Resurgence of Interest in Community Policing

In spite of the paucity of empirical data on which to base current police policies on the "order-maintenance" model or community-policing strategies, there has been a resurgence of interest in this policing strategy, and a recent increase in the number of programs initiated. This interest may be more a function of the failure of the "law-enforcement" or the "professional" model discussed earlier than an increase in support for this type of policing. Regardless of the reasons, significant attention and resources are being allocated to this phenomenon of community-oriented policing.

As discussed earlier, the community-policing model refers to police behavior which is responsive to situational and organizational factors that reflect the interpretations of community needs and expectations by the police. Several recent studies have examined this model of policing which is often seen as a response to a community or neighborhood mandate that something must be done about situations where formal institutions cannot or will not respond for a variety of reasons (Sykes, 1986). The major theme of the community policing model is increased interaction between the police and the community, or as discussed earlier, between the informal control system of the neighborhood and the formal control system of the police. The most common elements of this model include increased involvement of the community in getting the police job done, the permanent assignment of police officers to a neighborhood in order to cultivate better relationships with citizens, setting police priorities consistent with the specific needs and desires of the community, and meeting these needs by the allocation of police resources and personnel otherwise assigned to responding to calls for police assistance.

The purpose of the model is to achieve a greater emphasis on non-adversarial problem-solving in lieu of traditional strategies which conflict with normative structures in the neighborhood. Non-adversarial policing is achieved through the development of specific tasks and policing strategies which should be based upon a combination of law enforcement requirements, community needs, and techniques of crime prevention.

Perhaps the first major attempt in the 1980s to implement aspects of the community-oriented policing model was the State of New Jersey's "Safe and Clean Neighborhoods Program" (Wilson and Kelling, 1982). This program instituted foot patrols in twenty-eight New Jersey cities. Evaluations of the effectiveness of these foot patrols indicate that they did not reduce crime or victimization, but they did make citizens feel safer and they did maintain order in the communities they patrolled. Further, the officers had higher levels of job satisfaction than other officers.

Greene and Taylor (1987:22) review eight community policing strategies implemented in several cities which have been evaluated. These include:

1. The Flint Foot Patrol Project (Trojanowicz, 1986)
2. The First Newark Foot Patrol Experiment (Police Foundation, 1981)
3. The Second Newark Foot Patrol Experiment (Williams and Pate, 1987)
4. The Oakland Diversified Patrol Strategy Intervention (Reiss, 1985)
5. The San Diego Community Profile Project (Boydstun and Sherry, 1975)
6. The Houston Fear Reduction Program (Brown and Wycoff, 1987)
7. The Boston Foot Patrol Project (Bowers and Hirsch, 1987)
8. The Baltimore County Project COPE (Cordner, 1987)

In their review, Greene and Taylor (1987:36–37) conclude that there is not much consistency in findings across the studies; the results of the studies disagree on the effectiveness of foot patrols in reducing crime. Similar inconsistencies are reported in the findings regarding the reduction of the fear of crime. Most studies revealed no drop in crime as a result of foot patrols. However, because of the methodological deficiencies of the evaluations, Green and Taylor state that it is inappropriate to suggest that community policing and foot patrols do not work. They suggest additional research that will correct some of the conceptual and methodological deficiencies in the eight studies. Beyond these eight projects which have been studied, other undocumented community-oriented policing programs have no doubt been established with neither a strategic plan nor an evaluation. This research leaves us with not much more than cautious optimism for the benefits of community policing.

Herman Goldstein (1987) bases his argument for a more complete return to community-oriented policing on recent research findings which have questioned the value of traditional policing methods. He argues that the traditional method is too restrictive in over-emphasizing law-enforcement functions when many of the nonenforcement functions are extremely important for the effect they have on the quality of life in a community. He claims that many of the new experiments with community-oriented policing are based upon a better understanding of the capacity and complexity of the police function that has been acquired in recent years (Goldstein, 1987:7).

Goldstein also points out some important distinctions between the older community-policing projects and those that have been launched within the past several years in this country. The newer projects have been started at the initiative of the police in an attempt to improve the quality of police services, rather than primarily as a means of giving the community more direct control over police operations (Goldstein, 1987:7–8). Further, the newer projects grow out of a more solid understanding of police operations and research evaluating their effectiveness than was available in the past.

Jack Greene explains a number of the key issues of community policing in his introduction to a special issue of the *American Journal of Police*.

In recent years there has been a resurgence of interest in programs that attempt to place the police and the community in greater harmony and interaction. Many large and medium sized cities have adopted variations of "community policing" programs, each of which emphasize some combination of crime reduction and prevention, increased community cohesion and informal social control, and fear reduction policing strategy (1987:1).

Greene emphasizes that the "new" community policing movement is attempting to clarify the relationship between the formal and informal systems of social control, which stresses our interactive framework.

Skolnick and Bayley (1986), in their book, *The New Blue Line: Police Innovation in Six American Cities*, review the research evaluating traditional strategies to crime control. These strategies include increasing the number of police, random motorized patrolling, two-person patrol cars, saturation patrolling, improving response time to emergency calls, and improving techniques for criminal investigation. The authors indicate that the primary strategies followed by American police departments are neither reducing crime nor reassuring the public (Skolnick and Bayley, 1986:5–6). This conclusion has resulted in a new thrust in American policing:

The new thrust in American policing, which we loosely designate community-oriented policing, is not a single coherent program. Rather, police forces around the country are experimenting with a variety of new programs all resting on the rationale, not always clearly articulated, that police must involve the community in a practical way in the police mission (Skolnick and Bayley, 1986:211).

In most situations, the experiments with community-policing strategies are based on gut feelings or opinions of police administrators. While this has merit, a purpose of the present study is to begin developing a base of empirical data that can be used to direct these new programs. The question remains, how do we begin building closer police-community interaction without a greater understanding of unique characteristics of specific communities? What are the basic values and norms of specific communities, and how can police strategies address and synchronize with those characteristics? We must be familiar with the makeup of the informal social control system of specific neighborhoods in order to devise a community-based strategy.

In sum, there has been a substantial resurgence of interest in community policing. Subsequently, there have been a number of studies which have attempted to assess the effects of community policing strategies. The results of these evaluations are incomplete and inconclusive at the present time. None of the studies we have located has the benefit of an adequate conceptual or analytical framework. These community-policing programs have been established upon weak theoretical bases, and as a result of the failure of traditional policing strategies. After these programs are initiated, there is a tendency for them to take on a life of their own and begin to increase their span of control, a typical pattern for bureaucratic growth. Unfortunately, this process of metamorphosis occurs without adequate empirical support or direction.

The general purpose of the Miami study is to create a model for establishing community-specific policing strategies. This empirically-based model is founded upon a solid conceptual and theoretical framework.

Research Question

The specific purpose of this research is to examine the differences in agreement and disagreement with various police practices among the residents of ethnically-distinct neighborhoods in Miami, Florida. The findings should provide some needed empirical evidence for determining whether William F. Whyte was correct, and whether significant differences between neighborhoods really exist. Further, these findings can guide police training to meet citizens' expectations for acceptable and effective policing. Research comparing ethnically-distinct neighborhoods has not fully examined this aspect of neighborhood influences on policing. However, Michael K. Brown's study of police officers working the street found this to be an important aspect of police work. Police officers "fashion a coherent set of beliefs to guide their actions. These beliefs structure their perception of events and their definition of the situation, and provide the norms and standards that influence their judgment of alternative courses of action" (1981:7). Brown describes the major influences of police behavior as: (1) knowledge of the community; and (2) his or her interpretation of the community's expectations of how the police should act (Brown, 1981:56).

It is our expectation that communities vary considerably in the expectations residents have for police services. Residents of various culturally-distinct neighborhoods may have different values dictating the appropriateness of police behavior and of the policing styles used in specific situations. These preferences and dislikes are interwoven into the fabric of the culture, the attitudes toward general authority, and more specifically toward police authority. In turn, police strategies and practices incongruent with the basic culture and values of a neighborhood would likely be ineffective and perhaps even counterproductive to maintaining order and controlling crime.

Our goal is to initiate an exploration into empirical justifications for community-specific strategies of policing. To place our study in its proper perspective, our next section describes Dade County, the area in which our study was conducted, and includes a brief sketch of recent police-citizen confrontations which have affected police-community relations.

2

The Socio-Cultural Context of Police-Citizen Relations in Dade County, Florida

Dade County, Florida, is a unique county. There are many aspects of Dade County that resemble no other county in the United States. The 1,955 square-mile tract of land has been referred to as Paradise, Paradise Lost, Paradise Found, the Murder Capital of the United States, the Cocaine Capital of the United States, and Home of the Most Bloody F.B.I. Shootout in History, among other complimentary and not-so-complimentary names. It is a demographic phenomenon; it is not Middletown, U.S.A. Dade County and Miami are characterized by the media with scenes from Miami Vice and Scarface, by reports of its beautiful beaches and its illicit drug trafficking. Miami is at least tri-ethnic; it is one of the only American cities to experience race riots in the 1980s.

There were at least 1,796,000 people in Dade County as of 1985, and that includes only the legal, daytime residents. It is estimated that another 100,000 people live outside the county but work in Dade. During the winter months millions of tourists visit Dade County, and thousands of snowbirds take up part-time residence. In 1980, more than 100,000 Cubans immigrated to South Florida, and 25,000 Haitians took refuge on its shores. No study of Dade County's population would be realistic without considering these two major events. Our best estimates, however, break down the population at the time of our research (in 1985), and are presented in Table 2-1. This is a

Table 2-1.
Population of Dade County, 1985

Ethnic	Number	%
Anglo	661,000	37
Black	367,000	20
Hispanic	768,000	43
Total	1,796,000	100

dramatic change from 1970, when the Anglo population was 67 percent, the blacks were 16 percent of the population, and Hispanics accounted for 17 percent of the 1,167,792 residents.

In 1985, 47 percent of the population was male and 62 percent was between 18 and 64, while 15 percent of the population was 65 or older. More than 628,000 residents have settled in Dade County between 1970 and 1985, and it is the Hispanic and elderly who make up a large percent of this increase. More than 10 percent of the total labor force was unemployed in 1983, and 11.9 percent of the population was living below the national poverty level. The official population projection for 1990 is 1,894,500, and only time will tell whether that projection is accurate, and what characteristics the 100,000 new residents will possess.

It is difficult to say what impact the changing face of Dade County has had on its social institutions. There is a long and complicated history which explains why the social fabric in Dade County has been worn so thin. This particular history includes maneuvers and racial tensions based upon the voting strength and power of the various ethnic/interest groups. If the population of Dade County becomes dominated by powerful Hispanics, as the trends indicate, then the war may be over. For the time being, however, the battles rage on (see Reiff, 1987).

POLICE IN DADE COUNTY

There have been numerous battles fought in Miami and Dade County. Some have been in the political arena, yet some have been on the streets. Most have been over racial issues. Although the history of Dade County is fascinating, only the history of police and the community is relevant to our study (Buchanan, 1977). A review of police and the community must include a chronological report of riots in the streets.

The Miami Riot in 1968 was similar to other major racial riots which took place during the 1960s. It occurred during the same week that the Republican National Convention in Miami Beach nominated Richard Nixon for president. While there was no direct link between the Republican Convention and the riot, it is believed that the presence of the Republicans inspired several black political groups to organize political rallies. One of these rallies was scheduled in Liberty City for 1 P.M. on August 7, 1968. As the crowd grew and overflowed from the Community Center into the street, tempers flared and according to reports, the unkept promises of the white community apparently festered in the minds of the black youth. No one can say who threw the first stone, but when a white man driving a pickup truck with a "George Wallace for President" sticker on the bumper drove by, the Miami riot of 1968 was started. After three days of rioting, with 950 national guardsmen called in to control the situation, four black men were dead.

Between 1970 and 1979, Dade County experienced fourteen outbursts of racial violence. These disturbances were caused by activities ranging from bad meat in a grocery store to excessive use of police force. There were many other incidents in Dade County which could have caused race riots but did not. Perhaps these incidents built up the anger in the minds and hearts of black citizens in Dade County, and contributed to the rage which occurred in 1980, known as the McDuffie riots.

ARTHUR MCDUFFIE

On December 16, 1979, Arthur McDuffie, a divorced thirty-three-year-old black insurance agent went to run some errands on a Kawasaki 900 motorcycle. After his errands and a visit with a female friend, McDuffie headed home sometime around 1 A.M. The exact sequence of events after a Metro-Dade police officer spotted McDuffie is disputed. What is known is that there was a high-speed pursuit, a fight, and when it ended, McDuffie's head was split open and he died four days later. Several of the police officers involved engaged in a cover-up which was finally ended when four officers were charged with manslaughter and a fifth was charged for tampering with evidence. The trial was moved to Tampa and the officers were tried by an all-white jury. On May 17, 1980, the jury returned its verdict after just two hours and forty-five minutes of deliberation. At 2:42 P.M. the news hit Miami and the rest of the country. Many Miamians, both black and white, were shocked by the acquittals. For the black community, the significance of the trial went far beyond the McDuffie case. It represented the status of blacks in the criminal justice system; it demonstrated that all their grievances, all their distrust in the system, all the racist beliefs, suddenly turned out to be true.

All afternoon on May 17, crowds were growing and people were voicing their anger toward the verdict, toward the criminal justice system and toward society in general. Around 5 P.M. the first rocks and bottles were thrown. From that moment, the riot escalated and spread with incredible speed. The government did everything in its power to calm the disturbance. Police and National Guardsmen were horribly unprepared and unorganized. This riot, unparalleled in modern American history for its random anti-white violence, ended after three days with eighteen dead, $80 million in property damage, and more than 1,100 people arrested.

THE AFTERMATH

The McDuffie riot created numerous problems for Dade County. The aftermath of the riot included prosecuting the rioters, obtaining riot relief, and reviewing the causes of race riots in 1980. Briefly, the criminal justice system was very lenient toward the rioters. Slightly more than 10 percent of all cases went through the system, and most of them were placed in some pretrial diversion project.

Shortly after the riot ended, local, state and federal agencies worked together and planned for a rebuilding of the areas which were hardest hit. It was thought that the riot-torn area would be cleared, rebuilt and an economic recovery plan created for the black community. It was hoped that housing, recreation and employment opportunities would be created or expanded. Black leaders were also promised more governmental representation.

Expectations were raised; local, state and federal agencies set up study groups and Blue-Ribbon panels, millions of dollars were pumped into the community, but as we found out, it takes more than money to solve the social, political and economic problems of the black community in Miami. At that time, late 1980 and early 1981, the residents of Dade County and Miami were apparently ready for change and looked to governmental agencies and the private sector for leadership (Porter and Dunn, 1984). A survey conducted by the Dade-Miami Criminal Justice Council (1981:48) demonstrated that residents of Dade County were still confident in the performance of their police. This finding was somewhat surprising in light of the recent events. A full 87 percent of the residents reported that, in general, police were doing a good (49.4%) or average (36.6%) job. Only 48 citizens (14%) reported that the police were doing a poor job. When broken down by ethnicity, the survey results revealed that only 7 blacks (11.7%), 13 whites (10.7%), and 21 Hispanics (18.6%) reported a poor grade for police. Conversely, 21 blacks (35.0%), 96 whites (57.1%) and 53 Hispanics (43.9%) gave the police a good evaluation. More than three times as many blacks reported a good score for police than a poor score. Due to the current problems and the major riot, this level of support for the police was encouraging.

Information about the attitudes of community members was being gathered at several levels on various issues. This information made it apparent that one method of reducing the discontent would be to initiate programs to rebuild the area and increase its business potential. During the months and years after the 1980 riot, some new businesses were loaned sufficient money to settle in Liberty City (the main area torn by the riot). There were, however, more promises than action! The U.S. Civil Rights Commission (1982) investigated the situation and published a lengthy report, and numerous state and local task forces made hundreds of recommendations and suggestions.

The local governmental response was, in part, to initiate changes in the police departments. The bottom line was to improve police procedures, attitudes and public relations. There were major changes made in the recruitment, selection and training of police officers, including the promoting of minority officers to command-level positions.

BEYOND THE AFTERMATH

The U.S. Civil Rights Commissions's *Confronting Racial Isolation in Miami* was issued in June, 1982. This report focused on the plight of the black in Dade County, emphasizing problems in education, housing, economic development, employment and the juvenile and criminal justice systems. The report's general recommendation is "The public and private sectors of the Miami-Dade community should work together to develop a long-term coordinated attack on the underlying causes of racial isolation and exclusion" (1982:317). This recommendation was followed by more specific suggestions to aid the plight of the black in Miami. In fact, in the preface of the report, it was noted that the underlying causes of black or white violence are present in most depressed inner-city communities, and that the anger, frustration, fear and hopelessness expressed by the blacks in Miami are identical to those documented in studies of disturbances in other cities.

This report angered members of the black community and increased their alienation and deepest fear that little would be done to improve their lot. More meetings were held and more talking was done, but the same problems which caused the riot, the same festering problems of housing, unemployment, education, recreation, economic development, and a perceived unfair criminal justice system persisted.

OCTOBER 6, 1982

It is impossible to say whether or not the black community was satisfied with the progress that had been made. Although no major, single event can be identified as an indicator (in either direction), there continued to be a great deal of tension within the black community. On October 6, 1982, however, an event took place which can be identified as a turning point.

Officer Thomas Pellechio, an Anglo police officer, driving an unmarked car, made a routine traffic stop. He stopped Ernest Kirkland, a black corrections officer. The encounter escalated into a fight and ended with Pellechio shooting Kirkland four times. On October 26, 1982, a Latin police officer accidently shot and killed a young black male. These two shootings of black males raised more than a few eyebrows in the black community. But it was a shooting on December 28, 1982 that sent the rioters back to the streets.

On December 28, 1982, a young Hispanic police officer, Luis Alvarez, was patrolling the Overtown area of Miami. He was acting as a field-training officer, and was teaching his young recruit Luis Cruz. The officers entered a video parlor which was known as a "drugstore" and walked through. Just as they were about to leave, Officer Alvarez noticed a bulge in the shirt of a young black playing a video game. Alvarez approached the young man and asked him to identify the bulge. Nevell Johnson answered, "a gun." As the officers were arresting Johnson, he apparently turned reaching for his gun. Officer Alvarez fired once, killing Johnson.

A crowd of angry black youths gathered outside the video parlor as police rushed to remove Officers Alvarez and Cruz, and take Johnson to the hospital. In a fashion similar to the 1980 riots, the crowd grew, rocks and bottles began to fly and by nightfall of December 28, 1982, there was another riot in Miami. For three days, thousands of black rioters clashed with police. Although this riot was not as bloody as the one in 1980, the hatred, fear and distrust surfaced in a similar fashion. The death of Nevell Johnson, as with the death of Arthur McDuffie, became a symbol of racial disharmony in Miami. Officer Alvarez was soon indicted for manslaughter and apparently sacrificed to the black community for peace and harmony. An all-out effort was made to prosecute Alvarez, and he was convicted in the media before the trial date was even set.

Tension in the black community was at an all-time high, and the sacrifice of Officer Alvarez to the black community seemed a small price for relative peace and tranquility. The political community reacted to the situation as predicted, by establishing study groups and task forces to investigate and report on the plight of the black in Overtown. The U.S. Civil Rights Commission was asked to examine the situation in Miami again; this time only months since its last report was issued.

The year 1983 was a rough one for Dade County, Miami and its police departments. During the six-month period between November, 1982 and May, 1983, eight police officers killed civilians. Four officers were indicted and four officers were clearly justified in the other incidents (Alpert, 1989). Regardless of the reasons, the large number of shootings outraged the community. Several groups decided to study the reasons behind the shootings including the City of Miami, which established an Overtown Blue Ribbon Committee (1984) and the Dade County Grand Jury (1983).

The Overtown Blue Ribbon Committee, although created, in part, because of the Alvarez shooting, avoided any discussion of a particular incident. Instead, that group focused upon many of the same issues as the U.S. Civil Rights Commission Report. Many of the specific observations and recommendations were similar. In addition, a major conclusion of this report is that "The actual or perceived use or misuse of political power and the manipulation of minority-group conflicts contribute to racial unrest in Miami" (1984:169). This recommendation is consistent with the public's concern over the political situation in Miami; each ethnic group was used against the other for the advancement of someone's political career. It fit well with the concern that Officer Alvarez may, indeed, be sacrificed to pacify the black community.

The other report, issued by the Dade County Grand Jury, noted that police officers' behavior and attitudes were at an all-time low, and that the publics' perception of the police was equally dismal. The report called for dramatic changes in police selection and training. The major thrust of this report was aimed at the reduction of police-citizen violence. The critical view of police by the watch-dog group was well received by all segments of Greater Miami. It was hoped that the sum total of these reports would speed the reform efforts of the police.

All of this activity may have been successful in calming down the angry citizens, had the manslaughter trial of Officer Luis Alvarez ended as the media was reporting it. In fact, the media coverage of the nine-week trial directed the expectations of the community. The full resources of the State's Attorney's Office were used to convict Officer Alvarez. Had it not been for a brilliant defense attorney, Roy Black, and his expert assistance, the problems of civil disturbances in Miami might have ended.

The evening of March 15, 1984, after slightly less than an hour of deliberation, the all-white jury returned a verdict of not guilty. What followed was probably the only predictable riot in American history. The police had been warned of the imminent riot if the jury acquitted Officer Alvarez. Upon the reading of the verdict, blacks hit the streets throwing bottles, rocks, and looting as well. Fortunately, the police were prepared and ended the disturbance after only one evening and part of the next day of rioting.

Since the Alvarez shooting, several significant events have taken place affecting Miami and Dade County law enforcement. The Miami police chief (an Anglo), Kenneth Harms, was fired at 2:47 A.M. on January 27, 1984, by the black city manager, Howard Gary. Several months later, the city manager was fired by the City Commission. Since then, several police chiefs have been appointed to head the Miami police, but to date, the management, supervision, and control of the Miami Police Department lacks direction. In fact, the management, supervision and control of the City of Miami is being directed by members of its city commission who have been fighting among themselves for years. The former mayor, a major brawler himself, was quoted (August 23, 1985), in the *Miami Herald* as stating:

The problem is we have a commission filled with Clint Eastwoods . . . one wants to be Dirty Harry. Another wants to play The Good, the Bad and the Ugly and the other wants to play Fistful of Dollars. We are getting government by Clint Eastwood cliché.

One commentator aptly noted that the Mayor appears to be living "Cougan's Bluff." Maurice Ferre, who had been elected Mayor of Miami in six consecutive elections, lost in September, 1985 to Xavier Suarez. To make matters worse, more than twenty police officers were arrested between 1984 and 1986, on charges ranging from possession of cocaine to murder, and in 1985, a federal grand jury initiated an investigation on many high-ranking police officers.

Most of the other twenty-six police departments in Dade County, including the largest and most visible—the Metro-Dade Police Department—all suffered various degrees of disorder and disruption. Although the situation has greatly improved since the immediate aftermath of the McDuffie riots, many problems, or at least the perception of problems, lingered into the mid-1980s.

The police administrators, in an effort to improve policing, have encouraged several major studies and research efforts to investigate public opinion, officers' morale, and crime-reporting trends, among other issues. In addition, in 1985 the Metro-Dade Police Department funded two studies, one to the Police Foundation to explore ways to reduce police-citizen violence, and another, this present study, to investigate policing in a multi-ethnic community.

3

Methods of Data Collection

We turn now from the rather abstract conceptual and theoretical issues discussed in Chapter 1 to a more specific discussion of the Miami study. Miami has become one of the most important laboratories for sociological studies on many issues due to its rich ethnic demographic composition and its recent Latin immigration. A combination of historical and recent events has created a rapidly changing cosmopolitan center with a distinct international composition that has been thrust into the role of being the crossroads between North and South America.

In the first section of this chapter, we discuss the design for the Miami study, including the selection of the study neighborhoods. The second section is devoted to a description of the types of data we collected.

SELECTION AND SAMPLING WITHIN
NEIGHBORHOODS

The Miami study is a sample of neighborhoods and a sample of individuals within neighborhoods. Each sample was chosen to allow us to study most advantageously the issues central to our concerns—the relationships between the police and communities. The sample of neighborhoods was designed to allow comparisons between areas with high versus low crime rates and distinct ethnic and social class compositions. Consistent with our sampling theory, we selected samples randomly within neighborhoods to assure generalizability at the neighborhood level, our unit of study. We did not select the samples to represent Dade County residents. This sampling technique allows us to study how individual attitudes and experiences accumulate to produce the aggregate patterns unique to the neighborhood.

Neighborhoods were selected because of their uniqueness, rather than to represent a balanced cross section of Dade County. Indeed, the overall population of Dade County is so segmented by ethnicity and social class that any overall characterization of the population would be difficult, if not impossible.

With the assistance of police officials and 1980 census data, we chose five unique neighborhoods out of a larger number of possibilities. The following neighborhoods were selected for the study:

1. *Rolling Oaks.* Rolling Oaks is a relatively small community of about 150 recently-built homes. Almost all of the residents are upper middle-class blacks, most of whom are professionals. To complete a sample of fifty homes, every third house was sampled.

2. *James Scott Housing Project.* The James Scott Housing Project is a government subsidized housing project for low-income blacks. There are a total of 858 units, most of which are occupied (837). This neighborhood was involved in most of the race riots described in chapter one. Since the last riots, a team-policing program was established which stationed police officers (volunteers) within the project to work closely with the director and his staff, and the residents. With the institution of the team-policing approach, it is hoped that police-citizen trust is being restored in a gradual but significant pattern. Every sixteenth unit was sampled to complete a sample of fifty units.

3. *1960 Cuban Entrants.* The third neighborhood is a combination of middle-class and working-class homes so characteristic of Miami. It contains a very high percentage of Latin residents, most of whom are Cubans who immigrated during the first wave of Cuban immigration in the 1960s. This group immigrated to South Florida as a result of the revolution in Cuba and the following Communist insurgency. Most of the Cuban immigrants who participated in this airlift left behind their middle-class lifestyles and their personal belongings to start a new life in America. The group's economic as-

similation was very rapid, but most of them continue to retain their culture and language.

In the neighborhood selected to represent this group, there were nearly 700 homes. Every fourteenth residence was chosen to yield a sample of fifty homes.

4. *1980 Cuban Entrants.* The procedure used to sample the fourth neighborhood represents an attempt to identify the attitudes of a new group of Cuban immigrants in the Miami area. The police identified a neighborhood where many Mariels (Cuban entrants who were part of the 1980 boatlift) lived. It was predominantly an area of apartments and condominiums. Interviewers were instructed to screen prospective subjects, for being Latin and having immigrated from Cuba in the Mariel Boatlift in 1980. A Mariel neighborhood was included in the study because of the tremendous impact the Mariels made on Miami. Given the overwhelming size of the Mariel boatlift and the fact that it was laced with hardened criminals and mental patients from Fidel Castro's institutions, some social disruption was inevitable. By the end of the boatlift, the equivalent of a city (approximately 92,000 Cubans) had been added to Dade County's population. Mariel refugees now represent one out of every eighteen persons in Dade County and one out of every seven Hispanics.

Interviewers selected every fifth household until they completed fifty interviews. During the year following the boatlift, Mariel refugees represented 16 percent of all felony arrests in Dade County, more than three times their proportion of the population (Dade County Grand Jury, 1982).

5. *Kendall Area.* The fifth neighborhood is a well-established Anglo middle and upper middle-class area. There were about 900 houses in the Kendall neighborhood we chose, so every eighteenth home was sampled to yield a total of fifty homes.

Each neighborhood unit was chosen to be included in the study because it represented a concentration of people with similar backgrounds, ethnicity, lifestyle and social status. Each was a locality with sentiments, traditions, and a history of its own. Each neighborhood was identifiable by these criteria to the police, city planners and to residents of Dade County. Most important, police administrators identified these areas as distinct neighborhoods for which more information was needed before they could institute effective neighborhood-specific strategies.

The data in Table 3-1 summarize the ethnic and gender distributions of each neighborhood sample. We can see the dis-

Table 3-1.
Ethnic and Gender Composition of Neighborhood Samples

	Male	Female	Anglo	Black	Hispanic	Other
Rolling Oaks	57%	43%	0%	96%	2%	2%
James Scott	38%	63%	0%	98%	0%	2%
1960 Cubans	78%	22%	0%	0%	100%	0%
1980 Cubans	73%	27%	0%	0%	100%	0%
Kendall	78%	22%	87%	0%	11%	2%
Number of Cases	150	94	40	94	105	3
Total Percent	61%	39%	17%	39%	43%	1%

tinct ethnic nature of each of the neighborhoods. Rolling Oaks and James Scott are almost exclusively black. The 1960 Cuban and Mariel areas are exclusively Latin. The Kendall area is mostly Anglo, with a few Hispanics. There are no current data available to test the adequacy of the samples. Census data are five years old, and there has been considerable movement in and out of most of these areas during the last five years. The Marielitos are now immigrants within that time, and Rolling Oaks has been constructed within the five year period.

The neighborhoods sampled were homogeneous with respect to income (see Table 3-2). An analysis of variance indicates that there is significantly more variation among neighborhoods than within neighborhoods. The standard deviations indicate variation that is typical of income distributions, due to extreme scores on the high and low ends of the distributions. In an attempt to omit the outlying or extreme scores, we calculated inter-quartile ranges. These ranges are considerably lower, and in fact indicate considerable homogeneity within the majority of residents in each neighborhood sample. The inter-quartile ranges for the James Scott and 1980 Mariel neighborhoods are almost nonexistent.

A sampling procedure was developed to select the member of the household to be interviewed to insure a representative sampling of individuals living within households. We sampled only adults eighteen years of age and older, since our school survey sampled high school students in the areas. The procedure was to ask for the number of adults living in the household and the number of men and women. With this information the interviewer could select from a random table the adult to be interviewed: oldest woman, youngest man, etc. If the interviewer could not contact the selected person in one household after two visits, he substituted categories that were underrepresented. On the average, substitutions were made on 15 percent of the households. An exception to this was in the Mariel area where most of the targeted people were the only possible choice in their household. Our procedure also allowed substituting households after a second visit where no one was home. The interviewer would substitute once to the right and then the next time to the left. About 40 percent of the house-

Table 3-2.
Analysis of Variance of Income by Neighborhoods

	Mean	S.D.	N	Range	InterQuartile Range
Rolling Oaks	28.7	16.1	44	10-90	20-31
James Scott	6.1	6.0	49	0-31	3-6
1960 Cubans	15.8	8.3	50	5-36	10-19
1980 Cubans	10.4	7.1	50	5-52	7-9
Kendall	26.5	18.5	27	8-99	16-27
Total	16.3	14.2	220		

Significance = .0000
Significantly different pairs (1-2, 3, 4) (2-1, 4, 5) (5-2, 3, 4)

holds were substitutions. We are not very concerned about any resulting sampling bias because of the homogeneity of each of our neighborhoods.

Student Sample

A sample of high school students was selected to be used in some of the analyses. Five high schools were chosen to be surveyed, one from each of the five neighborhoods. Required courses for juniors and seniors were selected to ensure that most juniors and seniors had equal chances of being in the sampled classes. We then sampled enough classes to obtain 80 to 100 subjects per school.

In Table 3-3 the schools are listed by ethnicity. Northwestern is almost exclusively black and Carol City is mostly black with a few Hispanics. Coral Park is almost exclusively Hispanic with a few Anglos. Killian is mostly Anglo with a few blacks and Hispanics. American High School is a mixture of blacks, latins and Anglos.

We surveyed a total of 451 students (Killian, 87; Carol City, 90; American, 93; Coral Park, 80; Northwestern, 101). We used several gimmicks to get the attention and cooperation of the students. We took along a local University of Miami football star as an assistant and entertained some challenges to arm wrestle. All in all, we seemed to have very good cooperation on the part of students, both in completing the questionnaire and in the quality of responses. Instances where questions were not completed or were completed incorrectly were relatively few. Only 17, or 3.9 percent, of the student questionnaires were not usable. We will speak a little more about the quality of the data when we discuss the factor analysis of the attitude questions.

The data in Table 3-4 summarize the ethnic and gender composition of each school sample. We can see that the samples correspond very closely with the actual school populations with regard to ethnicity (compare Table 3-2 and Table 3-3).

Police Sample

The Metropolitan Dade County Police Department was formerly the Dade County Sheriff's Office. The department has

Table 3-3.
Gender and Ethnic Composition of the High Schools According to Enrollment Figures

	Male	Female	Anglo	Black	Hispanic	Other	Total Enrollment
American H.S.	50%	50%	23%	45%	31%	<1%	2216
Carol City H.S.	51%	49%	6%	76%	18%	<1%	1777
Coral Park H.S.	49%	51%	14%	>1%	85%	<1%	2131
Killian H.S.	50%	50%	62%	21%	14%	3%	2718
Northwestern H.S.	48%	52%	<1%	99%	<1%	0%	1954

Table 3-4.
Gender and Ethnic Composition of the School Samples

	Male	Female	Anglo	Black	Hispanic	Other
American	62%	38%	18%	48%	30%	4%
Carol City	24%	76%	3%	66%	26%	5%
Coral Park	42%	58%	16%	1%	78%	5%
Killian	30%	70%	67%	10%	14%	9%
Northwestern	44%	56%	1%	95%	3%	1%

jurisdiction over all unincorporated areas of Dade County, including urban, rural and suburban areas. Twenty-six other departments are responsible for the incorporated areas. The department has over 2,000 sworn officers divided into seven police districts.

Metro-Dade conducts one-day quarterly training sessions continuously over a three-month period. All officers and sergeants are required to attend a one-day session during each quarter. Districts schedule two or three officers each day to attend the sessions throughout the three-month period, which results in a pretty good representative sample of officers within districts.

We sampled officers attending quarterly training over a two-week period, which included about one-sixth of the entire force. Six officers failed to complete the questionnaire correctly or completely. Our usable sample is 295.

The data in tables 3-5 and 3-6 indicate that our sample did represent the entire population of Metro-Dade police officers quite closely. The proportions of subjects in the districts are comparable between the sample and the population. Male and female breakdowns are very close when comparing the sample with the population, as are the ethnic, age and experience comparisons.

VARIABLES AND MEASURES

In order to determine the attitudes toward the police and policing held by the many groups we were interested in, we conducted an exhaustive review of the research literature. Of course, there are numerous studies on the interrelationship between the police and the community, with numerous arrays of questions concerning attitudes toward the policing. We selected scales and sets of questions that were relevant to our research and that had stood the test of time with regard to reliability and validity testing. This set of over 150 questions, then, was given to the Metro-Dade Police command staff for review. The command staff made comments on the interpretation and wording of the questions as well as their relevance to our task. After gaining this conceptual confirmation, we se-

Table 3-5.
Police District Samples and Total Population Comparisons
(Officers and Sergeants)

	Population		Sample	
	N	%	N	%
Northeast	135	16.0%	24	13.6%
Central	120	14.3%	24	13.6%
Midwest	121	14.4%	27	15.2%
South	113	13.4%	30	16.9%
Southwest	156	18.5%	35	19.8%
Northeast	107	12.7%	24	13.6%
Airport	90	10.7%	13	7.3%
Total	842	100.0%	117	100.0%
Unassigned	1198	58.7%	101	36.3%

Table 3-6.
Police District Samples and Total Population

	Population		Sample	
	N	%	N	%
Gender				
Male	1729	85.0%	237	86.0%
Female	311	15.0%	39	14.0%
Ethnicity				
Anglo	1355	66.0%	170	62.0%
Black	402	20.0%	40	15.0%
Latin	276	14.0%	59	21.0%
Other	7	.3%	5	2.0%
Average Age	33		34	
Average Years Exp.*	7.7		9.99	

*Sample was asked total years experience whereas population statistics reflect years with Metro-Dade Department, which accounts for the slightly higher sample statistics.

lected the best set of questions out of the 150. In addition to assessing attitudes toward the police, we included brief scales that assessed attitudes toward other professionals in the criminal justice system (prosecutors, judges and attorneys). These scales were selected to allow a comparison to determine which subjects are negative or positive concerning the entire criminal justice system, of which the police are just a part. This allows an examination of the degree to which attitudes toward the police are independent from the more general attitudes about the entire criminal justice system. To extend this process of placing attitudes toward the police in the context of more general attitudes toward the larger institution (the criminal justice system) we included a scale assessing one's attitudes toward the major institutions in our society (financial, religious, political, mass media, etc.). This allows us to determine if a subject is extremely positive or negative toward the police because he is extremely positive or negative toward the entire criminal justice system or even the entire array of institutions in our society. Our study permits us to determine the generalizability of attitudes at three different levels: the police, the entire criminal justice system, and social institutions in general.

To accomplish this we collected five types of data on each of the seven samples (the five neighborhoods, the students and the police). The first type of data collected are background data, including demographic data and information about contacts with the police. The second type of data included thirty items assessing attitudes toward the police. The third type of data collected examine attitudes toward the criminal justice system, including police, prosecutors, judges and attorneys. The fourth type of data assess general attitudes toward major social institutions in America. Finally, the fifth type of data involve a specific set of questions asking subjects to place in priority criteria for evaluating the job performance of police officers.

Background Data

On the citizen questionnaire, we asked subjects in each of the five neighborhoods their length of residence, ethnicity (Anglo, black, Hispanic or other), education level, age, with whom they live and several questions concerning their contacts with the police and whether these contacts were positive or negative. Also, the citizens were asked about their employment, family income, and whether they received or are receiving public assistance. Finally, subjects were asked about ever being arrested.

High school students were asked questions about their gender, ethnicity (Anglo, black, Hispanic or other), with whom they live (both parents, mother, father or other) and about others in their household. Also, they were asked their grade in school, grade point average, length of residence, number of traffic tickets, number of other arrests, and whether they or family members have been a victim of a crime.

The police subjects were asked their district, current assignment, months in the district, number of years as a police officer and number of years in South Florida. In addition, they were asked their age, gender, ethnicity (Anglo, black, Hispanic or other), marital status and the highest grade completed.

ATTITUDES TOWARD THE POLICE
AND POLICING

These thirty questions were taken from the scales and indices assessing attitudes toward the police and policing we mentioned earlier. They include: Hostility Index, Attitudes toward the Police Questionnaire, Perceptions of Police Scale, Citizens Perception of Police (Brodsky and Smitherman, 1983), Police Aggressiveness Scale, Selectiveness of Law Enforcement, Perceived Limits on Discretion and Perception of Supervisor's Behavior, Patrolman's and Supervisor's Attitudes toward Aggressiveness, Patrolman's and Supervisor's Attitudes toward Order-Maintenance (Brown, 1981).

Many of these scales overlap or have very similar questions. Others had questions that were not appropriate for our study, so those questions were omitted. Our final thirty questions came from these scales, although some were altered slightly to make them more appropriate for our analysis or to make them easier to interpret.

FACTOR ANALYSIS

In the present study, the thirty items which were determined to be the most important were administered to 451 high school students, 296 police officers, and 250 Dade County residents. It was believed that certain specific attitudinal domains would emerge to form a combination of the 997 subjects. We wanted to reduce the total number of items, eliminate those which were highly correlated, and identify the concepts which were believed to be the most important by our subjects. In other words, we were looking for attitude domains which can be identified by groups of questions which are answered in patterned ways. Because individuals do not agree exactly in their judgments about police, we chose the factor analytic technique to detect such patterned deviations from the grand mean, and thereby identify the sets of questions which represent the most significant attitudinal domains. If no patterned deviations exist, factor analysis of our attitudinal data will produce about as many factors as there are questions.

Clearly patterned deviations will produce a much smaller number of factor dimensions than loosely patterned deviations by an analysis of both the slope and the response level. If, on the one hand, the patterns of deviation in the data have to do mainly with the level of response, all the stimulus values in a continuum ought to load on the same factor. This indicates that if an individual has a higher score than the group mean on one question, that he or she will tend to be high on all of the questions. If, on the other hand, slope differences predominate, the stimulus values from the extremes of a continuum should load in opposite directions, since a person who was higher than the group mean in the high range should also be lower than the group in the low range.

A factor analysis with a varimax rotation was performed on the scores of the thirty questions which were the most theoretically important to us and the Command Staff of the Metro-Dade Police Department. Separate factor analyses identified five distinct attitudinal domains for each of our sub-populations. Although several items emerged as more or less important among the sub-populations, our basic questions and attitudinal domains proved to be important across our total sample. The factor analysis for the total sample (977) revealed five factors (attitudinal domains) which included items with factor loadings greater than .50, which are presented in Table 3-7. There are two factor loadings, however, that are just under our .50 cutoff point (.47) that are included in factors three and five. These two exceptions were made because of the questions' conceptual congruence with the factors and because they were just below the cut-off limit. A factor loading is essentially the correlation between the original item and the composite factor. A factor loading approaching 1.0 indicates that the factor is practically identical with the original concept, and a factor loading of .00 means the specific variable or question contributes nothing to that particular factor.

Table 3-7.
Police Officer Task Evaluations

Questions	Factor: 1 Demeanor	2 Respon- sibil- ity	3 Neigh- borhood	4 Ethnic	5 Patrol
Police are usually courteous to people	.69	.01	-.08	-.05	.04
Most police officers are usually friendly	.69	.05	.01	-.03	-.06
Most police officers are usually rude	.68	-.11	-.09	-.15	-.06
Police officers enjoy kicking people around	.67	-.06	-.11	-.20	.09
Most police officers are usually fair	.66	.01	-.04	-.07	.08
Most police officers give people a chance to explain	.62	.05	-.01	-.06	.13
Police officers show concern when you ask them questions	.59	-.06	.10	-.06	.02
Most police officers usually respect me for who I am	.58	.13	-.03	-.06	.04
Only the police can control crime in Dade county	.04	.73	.02	.11	.09
Only the police can control crime in my neighborhood	.03	.70	.02	.07	.06
In order to prevent crimes and catch criminals, the police are sometimes required to stretch the search and seizure laws and other procedural safeguards	.12	-.01	.53	.06	.03
The police are more strict in some neighborhoods than in others	-.12	-01	.47	-.03	-.10
The police are justified in regarding a Hispanic as one who needs to be watched more than others	-.14	-.03	.01	.73	.03
The police are justified in regarding an anglo as one who needs to be watched more than other	-.16	.12	-.02	.60	.02
The police are justified in regarding a Black as one who needs to be watched more than others	-.11	.08	.17	.53	.10
In some neighborhoods, crime prevention requires that police officers stop people walking down the street and ask them where they are going or what they are doing	.29	.11	.08	.07	.50
A good police officer is one who patrols aggressively by stopping cars and checking people who look suspicious	.39	.19	.07	.12	.47

The Five Scales

Demeanor. This scale consists of seven items which measure the subject's perceptions of the general demeanor of police officers. Specific questions elicit responses concerning courteousness, friendliness, rudeness and concern or respect for citizens displayed by police officers. Statistically, this scale includes seven items measuring specific behaviors to represent a comprehensive measure of general demeanor. The lower the score, the stronger the perception of a positive demeanor.

Responsibility. This scale consists of two items concerning the role of the police in controlling crime: "only the police can control crime in Dade County/my neighborhood." The lower the score, the stronger the agreement with the statement that most of the responsibility for controlling crime rests with the police.

Discretion. Two questions are involved in this scale, which measures agreement with the need for variability in enforcing the law, and especially in stretching procedural safeguards in some neighborhoods or areas. The lower the score, the stronger the agreement with the need for variability in enforcement and in applying procedural safeguards.

Ethnic. This scale consists of three questions concerning the justification for suspicion of certain ethnic groups as being more crime prone. The three questions are identical except each makes reference to a different ethnic group: blacks, Hispanics and Anglos. The lower the score, the stronger the agreement with the idea that certain ethnic groups need to be watched more closely than others.

Patrol. Two questions comprise this scale, which measures the approval of active patrol strategies, such as stopping and questioning people walking down the street and stopping cars. The lower the score, the stronger the agreement that active patrol strategies are necessary to control crime.

Attitudes toward the Criminal Justice System

We selected a semantic differential instrument suitable for the specific purpose of assessing attitudes toward various aspects of the criminal justice system. More specifically, we focused on measuring the dispositional judgment related to the covert characteristics of professionals within the criminal justice system: police, prosecutors, judges and defense attorneys. The semantic differential is an instrument to assess connotative meaning. As the originators of the instrument described it,

the semantic differential is essentially a combination of controlled association and scaling procedures. We provide the subjects with a concept to be differentiated and a set of bipolar adjectival scales against which to do it, his only task being to indicate for each item (pairing a concept with a scale), the direction of his association and its intensity on a seven-step scale (Osgood, Suci and Tannenbaum, 1957).

The specific instrument with the specific choice of adjectival scales was selected from a study by James Sterling (1972). We used nine adjectival scales: cooperative-uncooperative, informed-uninformed, familiar-strange, fair-unfair, trusting-suspicious, good-bad, strong-weak, active-passive, important-unimportant. The scale was used to measure attitudes toward four groups of professionals in the criminal justice system: police, prosecutors, judges and attorneys. In analyzing the response of the subjects for each group, mean scores were calculated for each scale. The lower the score, the more positive the dispositional judgment concerning the characteristics of people in that group.

Attitudes toward Major Social Institutions

We questioned respondents about their confidence and trust in fifteen social institutions that have the greatest influence in their lives: banks, business companies, religion, education, medicine, the executive branch of government, federal government agencies, organized labor, the press, television, political parties, law enforcement, criminal courts, the U.S. Supreme Court and Congress. In addition to asking about confidence and trust in the general institution, we also asked about each institution as they encounter it in their lives, at the local or community level. For example, we asked about the institution of medicine, physicians in their community and their own doctor. For each question about a general institution, there was at least one about the local or community counterpart. Lipset and Schneider's work on confidence in institutions (1983) provided the framework for this set of questions. They argue that it is possible to construct a general index of confidence in institutions as a general phenomenon (Lipset and Schneider, 1983:97–98). They document a degree of consistency in the trends of confidence in different institutions over time. We questioned subjects on both feelings of confidence and trust (Lipset and Schneider, 1983:76) with a zero-to-five scale. Zero represents "total incompetence" and "can never be trusted." An average score was computed for each scale (competence and trust). The higher the score, the greater the competence and trust.

CRITERIA FOR EVALUATING THE JOB PERFORMANCE OF POLICE OFFICERS

We created a task-evaluation form which included crime-fighting performance measures, social service functions and other job-related duties which could be ranked by citizens as well as police officers.

We asked respondents to assess the degree of emphasis they felt should be placed on twenty different tasks when supervisors evaluate police officers. A ten point scale was used to assess the priority. A one represented a low emphasis and a ten represented a high emphasis. The twenty tasks included:

1. Report writing ability
2. Personal appearance
3. Judgment (taking appropriate action)
4. Initiative (works well without direct supervision)
5. Number of misdemeanor arrests
6. Number of traffic tickets
7. Number of felony arrests
8. Court presentation
9. Knowledge of procedures, laws, and court rulings
10. Human relations skills

11. Dependability (predictable job behavior, including attendance, promptness and reaction to stress and criticism)

12. Demeanor (professional attitude)

13. Ability to get along with other people

14. Being courteous

15. Have no complaints in one's file

16. Being active in community affairs

17. Have no personal or financial problems

18. Equal enforcement of the law

19. Making good discretionary decisions on the street

20. The use of excessive force to maintain a professional image.

In addition, we asked police officers their assessment of how supervisors do rate each of the twenty tasks in their current evaluation. This allows us to assess the differences between how officers think the tasks are rated and how they think they should be rated.

In the following three chapters, we apply the data we gathered to answer our major research question: what are the differences in agreement and disagreement with various police practices among the residents of ethnically-distinct neighborhoods. Each chapter addresses different measures of neighborhood norms concerning expectations towards policing, and the interaction between the formal and informal control systems. The next chapter focuses on ranking the importance of various police functions.

4

Police Task Evaluations

Just as citizens are observed by the police, police officers are watched and evaluated by community residents. This mutual observation serves as the basis of the police officers' knowledge of the community and the foundation of the community members' confidence and trust in the police officer. In modern-day police departments, technological advancements including the exclusive or expanded use of the automobile patrol have resulted in a corresponding decrease in familiarity with the unique characteristics of neighborhoods and their residents. This growing detachment, as well as other concerns which were discussed in Chapter 1, have spearheaded the movement among many police administrators and civic leaders to return to, or move toward, policing which is responsible and responsive to specific communities and neighborhoods. One of the most logical methods of designing strategies for the police is the coordination of law enforcement requirements with the preferences reported by the consumers of police service. This chapter will focus on community preferences for, and priorities assigned to, various police tasks. Specifically, we examine responses from the neighborhood residents and police officers regarding the

This chapter is a significantly revised version of G. Alpert and R. Dunham, "Community Policing," *Journal of Police Science and Administration* 14 (1986): 212–222.

priority of police tasks. In subsequent chapters, we discuss how the performance of these tasks should be used to evaluate the effectiveness of police officers and feed back into training modules.

Because successful police work requires that a number of extremely diverse tasks be accomplished by the same individual, it is little wonder that so much controversy exists over task priorities and evaluations based upon task performance. Police style is, in part, determined by the combined way in which a department and individual officer sort out these priorities. Police style had been a topic of only limited scholarly debate until William Westley (1953) studied individual styles of policing and James Q. Wilson (1968) clarified a typology of departmental police behavior. One of Wilson's major theses was that police departments can be classified into one of several types, which are influenced by community characteristics. Several years after Wilson's book was published, The National Advisory Commission on Criminal Justice Standards and Goals emphasized the importance of community characteristics when it noted (1973:13):

Because the responsibility of law enforcement and the provision of police services to meet local needs are properly borne by local government, it would be unrealistic to establish rigid criteria for all police agencies in the United States. Priorities regarding the police role are largely established by the community the police agency serves.

Since that time, others observed the wide variation in the behavior of police and attributed these differences to a number of factors (Meagher, 1985; Flanagan, 1985; Alderson, 1982; Whitaker et al., 1982; Muir, 1977). Adding to the traditional police and the community analysis, Michael Brown (1981:223) provides us with a good perspective on individual police officer styles and how to understand them. "A patrolman's operational style is based on his responses to . . . the difficulties and dilemmas he encounters in attempting to control crime . . . (and) the ways in which he accommodates himself to the pressures and demands of the police bureaucracy." Brown explains further that the officer's style derives from the specific choices he makes regarding the *selectivity* and *degree of aggression* used to work the street. Policing is affected by both the style of the organization, as influenced by the administration, and the style of individual officer, based upon certain distinctive features and traits.

An important and related issue involves the *effectiveness* of the various styles of policing in different communities. Research on police effectiveness and its variation among departments has been limited to the measurement of the general types mentioned above, the relationship between supervisors' expectations and police officers' attitudes and behavior (see Meagher, 1985 and Allen and Maxfield, 1983). As a result, this research has lacked an adequate multiple-indicator model (see McIver and Parks, 1983). There have been numerous attempts to improve police-community cooperation both by educating the public and by training the police.

Previous research using measures of police effectiveness has included such diverse criteria as: awards, complaints, sick leave and firearms removal (Bloch and Specht, 1973); supervisory ratings, activity levels, demeanor and attitude (Bloch and Anderson, 1974); peer ratings, job knowledge, dependability and human relations (Farr and Landy, 1979); academy grades, commendations and promotions (Spielberger et al., 1979) and tenure, marksmanship and accidents (Froemel, 1979). In other words, this prior research has been based upon a shotgun approach to measurement and has resulted in operationalizing police effectiveness based upon the numerous views of the police mission rather than any systematic approach (see Sharp, 1982 and Spielberger, 1979). One method by which citizens and the police can better understand each others' needs is to analyze how each ranks the relative importance of police tasks. Unfortunately, the ranking of specific performance tasks or criteria for evaluation by police and the public they serve has received insufficient attention (see Trojanowicz and Belknap, 1986). The research in this area is limited, and includes evaluations of police tasks as part of the literature on police stress (see Terry, 1981), the literature on the roles and functions of the police (see Bennett, 1983), and the police-community relations literature (see Klockars, 1985).

The only empirical study we located which focused directly

on police task evaluations was conducted in the late 1960s (Olson, 1970). This study was an early attempt to measure police activity preferences. In addition to ranking police task preferences, this type of research can indicate whether crucial differences exist among police officers and between the police and the public, and can suggest modifications in training.

In the early 1970s, Chief Dale Bowlin of the Metro-Dade (Florida) police department created an instrument to measure differences in task preferences among his patrol officers. He was concerned that the criteria by which the officers were being evaluated were not those by which the officers thought they should be evaluated. It was thought that if provided the opportunity, police officers would work to change their supervisors' perceptions and criteria for evaluation to benefit the consumer of police services. The results from Chief Bowlin's study indicated that supervisors' evaluations were weighting as the most important the crime-fighting performance measures and weighting as the least important the social service functions of police work (see Landy, 1977; Goldstein, 1977; and Allen and Maxfield, 1983).

From the results of the studies mentioned above, we created a list of twenty task evaluation criteria which includes crime-fighting performance measures, social service functions and other job-related duties which could be ranked by citizens as well as police officers. The list includes the following (in alphabetical order):

1. ability to get along with other people
2. appearance
3. being active in community affairs
4. complaints (have no complaints in one's files)
5. courteousness
6. court presentation
7. demeanor (professional attitude)
8. dependability (predictable job behavior, including attendance, promptness and reaction to stress and criticism)
9. discretion (making good decisions on the street)

10. equal enforcement of the law
11. felony arrests
12. force (use of excessive force to maintain an image)
13. human relations skills
14. initiative (works well without direct supervision)
15. judgment (taking appropriate action)
16. knowledge of procedures and laws
17. misdemeanor arrests
18. problems (have no personal or financial problems)
19. report writing
20. traffic tickets

The possible scores a respondent could assign to a particular task ranged from a low of 1 to a high of 10. Our findings will be reported in several ways. Since the mean scores represent relative values, and we located significant variations in the evaluation criteria among the various groups, our approach in presenting the data is to describe all of the differences and explain their importance. First, we will describe how the citizens ranked police activities within each neighborhood (within group differences), and then look at differences among the neighborhoods (between group differences).

Rolling Oaks

The data in Table 4-1 shows that the citizens of Rolling Oaks ranked knowledge (7.62), discretion (7.52), court presentation (7.46), dependability (7.39), courtesy (7.32), appearance (7.32), human relations skills (7.30), and the ability to get along (7.28) as the most important criteria by which police officers should be evaluated. These citizens also reported misdemeanor arrests (6.02), and issuing traffic tickets (6.08) as the least important tasks by which officers should be evaluated. It is evident that in this community, service is rated significantly higher than law enforcement.

Table 4-1.
Police Activity Rankings within Rolling Oaks

Activity	Mean	SD
Knowledge	7.62	2.30
Discretion	7.52	2.34
Court Presentation	7.46	2.27
Dependability	7.39	2.38
Courtesy	7.32	2.56
Appearance	7.32	2.09
Human Relations	7.30	2.44
Ability to Get Along	7.28	2.48
Felony Arrests	6.90	2.48
Equal Enforcement of the Law	6.88	2.62
Excessive Force of Image	6.88	2.62
Community Affairs	6.88	2.33
Judgment	6.84	2.48
Report Writing	6.82	1.88
Demeanor	6.76	2.47
Initiative	6.50	2.59
No Complaints	6.32	2.20
No Personal Problems	6.22	2.38
Traffic Tickets	6.08	2.63
Misdemeanor Arrests	6.02	2.49

Table 4-2.
Police Activity Rankings within James Scott

Activity	Mean	SD
Appearance	7.41	2.20
Judgment	7.02	2.78
Report Writing	6.77	3.14
Initiative	6.75	3.00
Discretion	6.53	3.29
Traffic Tickets	6.49	2.98
Misdemeanor Arrests	6.34	2.98
Felony Arrests	6.13	2.90
No Personal Problems	6.13	3.27
Excessive Force for Image	6.00	3.58
Equal Enforcement of the Law	5.57	3.48
No Complaints	5.56	3.40
Knowledge	5.55	3.43
Court Presentation	5.55	3.41
Dependability	5.23	3.54
Courtesy	5.22	3.18
Human Relations	5.22	3.11
Demeanor	5.02	3.19
Community Affairs	4.91	3.60
Ability to Get Along	4.87	3.01

James Scott

Residents of the James Scott Housing Project gave the lowest rankings of police activities of all the neighborhoods. The two criteria receiving the highest rankings were appearance (7.41) and judgment (7.02). The lowest rankings were given to one's ability to get along (4.87), involvement in community affairs (4.91), and the officers' demeanor (5.02). This neighborhood ranked the human service functions much *lower* than the duties of law enforcement.

1960 Cuban Entrants

Unlike the James Scott project residents, the 1960 Cuban immigrants gave extremely high rankings to all the police evaluation criteria. The data in Table 4-3 demonstrate that this group ranked knowledge with the highest possible mean score (10.00). Discretion (9.98), court presentation (9.90), and courtesy (9.84)

Table 4-3.
Police Activity Rankings within the 1960 Cuban Immigrants

Activity	Mean	SD
Knowledge	10.00	.00
Discretion	9.98	.14
Court Presentation	9.90	.46
Courtesy	9.84	.55
Judgment	9.78	.71
Demeanor	9.74	.88
No Personal Problems	9.70	.67
Ability to Get Along	9.70	.87
Felony Arrests	9.68	.98
Human Relations	9.58	.84
Initiative	9.40	1.34
Dependability	9.30	1.46
Equal Enforcement of the Law	9.16	1.81
Report Writing	9.12	1.60
Appearance	9.06	1.50
No Complaints	9.02	1.67
Misdemeanor Arrests	8.14	2.45
Excessive Force for Image	8.08	2.07
Community Affairs	8.02	2.47
Traffic Tickets	7.48	2.67

were not ranked far below. The lowest ranking was given to issuing traffic tickets (7.48), but it is important to note that this lowest ranking would be a high score in any of the non-Cuban groups. The most important evaluation criteria in this neighborhood is the service function.

1980 Cuban Entrants

This group of new arrivals to South Florida reported very high ratings for all of the evaluation criteria as listed in Table 4-4. The highest scores were given to judgment (9.52), having no personal problems (9.43), and court presentation (9.36). The lowest scores were given for misdemeanor arrests (6.98) and issuing traffic tickets (6.72). The residents from this neighborhood clearly ranked service criteria higher than law-enforcement tasks.

Table 4-4.
Police Activity Rankings within the 1980 Cuban Immigrants

Activity	Mean	SD
Judgment	9.52	1.16
No Problems	9.43	1.13
Court Presentation	9.36	1.48
Knowledge	9.32	1.90
Courtesy	9.26	1.84
Ability to Get Along	9.26	1.86
Human Relations	9.26	1.65
Initiative	9.18	1.83
Discretion	9.16	2.00
Demeanor	9.12	2.04
Felony Arrests	9.12	1.91
Report Writing	9.00	1.90
No Complaints	8.94	2.05
Dependability	8.74	2.10
Equal Enforcement of the Law	9.62	2.57
Appearance	8.44	2.37
Community Affairs	8.30	2.66
Excessive Force for Image	7.34	3.34
Misdemeanor Arrests	6.98	3.41
Traffic Tickets	6.72	3.58

Kendall

The data in Table 4-5 show that the Kendall residents ranked courtesy (8.94), demeanor (8.49), and judgment (8.41) as the most important criteria for evaluation, and issuance of traffic tickets (4.95) and misdemeanor arrests (5.00) as the least important police tasks. As in most of the other neighborhoods, the residents of Kendall rated the service function as more important than law-enforcement duties.

Citizens

Findings from the five different neighborhoods demonstrate that only minor within-group differences exist, but that significant differences in the reported priorities of police functions exist among the five neighborhoods. After a brief summary of these differences, our analysis will turn to a discussion of each specific function ranked by the members of the communities.

Table 4-5.
Police Activity Rankings within Kendall

Activity	Mean	SD
Courtesy	8.94	1.67
Demeanor	8.49	1.64
Judgment	8.41	1.98
Human Relations	8.33	1.84
Discretion	8.27	1.98
Knowledge	8.23	1.94
Ability to Get Along	8.20	2.07
Dependability	8.20	2.17
Initiative	8.00	3.54
Appearance	7.90	2.41
Court Presentation	7.19	2.23
No Complaints	6.96	2.04
Felony Arrests	6.63	2.80
Equal Enforcement of the Law	6.54	2.82
Community Affairs	6.44	2.33
No Problems	6.02	2.28
Report Writing	5.91	2.28
Excessive Force for Image	5.27	3.27
Misdemeanor Arrests	5.00	2.48
Traffic Tickets	4.95	2.58

The residents of Rolling Oaks rate the qualitative functions such as discretion, courtesy, and the ability to get along as much more important activities than issuing traffic tickets or making arrests. Residents who live in the James Scott Housing Project rate appearance and judgment as the most important criteria for police evaluations while they rate the ability to get along, involvement in community affairs and demeanor as the least important criteria for evaluating police performance. Residents from both the 1960 Cuban airlift and the 1980 Cuban Flotilla, as well as the residents of Kendall ranked traits such as having knowledge, using judgment and discretion as the most important criteria for evaluation, while tasks such as issuing traffic tickets and misdemeanor arrests were reported as the least important by members of these groups.

Our discussion of the police activities ranked by the citizens will follow the order in which they were asked in the questionnaire. The first activity was report writing. This activity received split ratings. Residents in both the Cuban neighborhoods rated this function as very important (but they rank more than one-half the criteria 9.00 or higher), while Kendall residents ranked it quite low. Appearance is a criterion that is important to the Cubans and ranked moderately important by the other groups. Police officers' judgment is important to both Cuban groups and Kendall residents. It is less important to the residents of the black neighborhoods. Initiative is a characteristic similar to that of judgment, and follows the same pattern of importance: high in the Cuban communities and Kendall, and lower in the black neighborhoods. Misdemeanor arrests and traffic tickets have similar rankings by the neighborhoods. Each is ranked relatively low by all the groups, but extremely low by residents of Kendall. Arrests for felonies is surprisingly low in all communities except the Cuban neighborhoods, which ranked most tasks in the high range. It is lowest in the James Scott projects. Court presentation follows a similar pattern of responses. This task is ranked high by the Cubans and very low by residents of James Scott. Knowledge received high marks from all the communities except James Scott. Human relations skills ranked high among the Cubans and Kendall residents, but surprisingly low among the black residents, especially those who live in James Scott. This pattern is true for dependability as well. Demeanor was reported to be very important to the 1960 Cuban immigrants, important to the 1980 Cuban immigrants and residents of Kendall, but not very important to the residents of the black communities, especially those from James Scott.

As demeanor, the ability to get along with people and being courteous to people is very important to the Cuban communities and Kendall residents, but is reported as less important for police evaluations by the residents of the black communities. Once again, James Scott residents rank these criteria lower in importance than residents of Rolling Oaks. Having no complaints filed against a police officer is most important to the Cubans, but not very important to the blacks or to Kendall residents. Involvement in community affairs receives generally low rankings by all neighborhoods. It is relatively important to residents of Rolling Oaks. Having personal problems is an important criterion for the residents of the Cuban communities. It received very low rankings from the residents of Kendall. Equal enforcement of the law was ranked quite high by the 1960 Cuban immigrants, as slightly less important by the 1980 Cuban immigrants, not very important by the residents of Rolling Oaks and Kendall, and hardly important at all by James Scott residents. Discretion is an important criterion to residents of the Cuban communities and Kendall but not as important to the residents of the black neighborhoods. The use of excessive force for image is only slightly important to any of the groups. It is ranked the highest by the 1960 Cuban immigrants and lowest by the residents of Kendall.

While differences among the neighborhood residents are significant, it is important to determine how police officers rank these functions and how they perceive their supervisors' rank ordering of them. In other words, the next section will review how the police rank these functions and tasks. This analysis will allow a comparison of police officer rankings with citizens' expectations of police functions, or the interaction between the formal and informal control systems.

Police

The data for the police officer sample are a little more sophisticated than what were collected from the citizens. Rankings by which police officers believe they *should be* evaluated by their supervisors, and how they believe they *are* evaluated were both collected. We will first describe these rankings and then analyze the difference scores. Next, we will look at differences among the officers and finally, we will report the results of a factor analysis of these task evaluations.

The data reported in Table 4-6 reveals that overall, police officers ranked judgment (8.70), initiative (8.45), dependability (8.44), discretion (8.41), and the ability to get along (8.27) as the most important tasks by which they should be evaluated. Other tasks such as demeanor (8.18) and human relations skills (8.15) are also seen as important performance criteria by which police should be evaluated. The performance tasks reported as least important for evaluation include involvement in community affairs (4.71), use of excessive force for image (4.80), issu-

Table 4-6.
Police Officer Task Evaluation

	How Officers Think They are Rated		How Officers Think They Should Be Rated		Mean Change	Should be Less Important		Should Remain the Same		Should be More Important	
	Mean	S.D.	Mean	S.D.		N	%	N	%	N	%
Report Writing	7.63	1.19	7.94	1.72	.33	42	14.2	169	57.1	85	28.7
Appearance	7.27	1.86	7.87	1.86	.79	30	10.1	158	53.4	108	36.5
Judgment	7.89	1.88	8.70	1.60	.79	21	7.1	152	51.4	123	41.6
Initiative	7.65	2.03	8.45	1.76	.86	25	8.4	139	47.0	132	44.6
Misdemeanor Arrest	6.28	2.65	5.34	2.39	-.94	109	36.8	118	39.9	69	23.3
Traffic Tickets	8.61	2.81	5.04	2.64	-1.58	126	42.6	105	35.5	65	22.0
Felony Arrests	6.74	5.94	5.94	2.41	-.80	107	36.1	121	40.9	68	23.0
Court Presentation	5.63	2.94	7.17	2.29	1.55	21	7.1	125	42.2	150	50.7
Knowledge	7.00	2.43	8.00	1.87	1.02	27	9.1	134	45.3	135	45.6
Human Relations Skills	7.14	2.43	8.15	1.87	1.02	30	10.0	130	43.9	136	45.9
Dependability	7.95	2.07	8.44	1.79	.49	38	12.8	157	53.0	101	34.1
Demeanor	7.57	2.14	8.18	1.82	.63	26	8.8	152	51.4	118	39.9
Ability to Get Along	7.67	2.00	8.27	1.81	.58	26	8.8	159	53.7	111	37.5
Courtesy	7.27	2.26	7.89	1.95	.58	32	10.8	145	49.0	119	40.2
No Complaints	6.74	2.88	5.99	3.02	-.78	95	32.1	123	41.6	78	26.4
Community Affairs	4.65	2.89	4.71	2.88	.11	57	19.3	156	52.7	83	28.0
No Personal Problems	4.75	3.10	5.23	3.17	.50	42	14.2	156	52.7	98	33.1
Equal enforcement of the Law	6.20	2.81	7.19	2.51	1.01	15	5.4	162	54.7	118	39.9
Discretion	7.29	2.41	8.41	1.86	1.11	15	5.1	149	50.3	132	44.6
Use of Force for Image	4.89	3.19	4.80	3.29	.06	49	16.6	181	61.1	66	22.3

ing traffic tickets (5.04), having personal problems (5.23), misdemeanor arrests (5.34), and felony arrests (5.94). These rankings indicate a clear preference for evaluative criteria that are service-oriented as opposed to those that measure enforcement of the laws. Police officers' ranking of these evaluation criteria indicate a desire to be judged on the basis of their service and reasonableness and not on the basis of a cold, empirical measure of performance.

Preferences are not always given the highest priority in evaluating police officers. In fact, the police officers in our study indicated that they think their evaluations are weighted heavily by measures of their dependability (7.95), judgment (7.89), ability to get along (7.67), initiative (7.65), report writing (7.63) and demeanor (7.57). They think their evaluations are weighted the least by their involvement in community affairs (4.65), lack of personal problems (4.75), use of excessive force for image (4.89), court presentation (5.63), and equal enforcement of the law (6.20). In general, the officers report that they are evaluated by criteria which are substantially different from those by which they believe they should be evaluated. Fortunately, three of the most important criteria for both categories are judgment, initiative and dependability.

Perhaps the best way to look at which criteria of evaluation are the most disjointed between how officers think they should be evaluated and how they think they are evaluated is to analyze the difference in mean scores. The measures with the largest mean difference are:

1. court presentation (1.55)

2. discretion (1.11)

3. human relations skills (1.02)

4. knowledge (1.02)

5. equal enforcement of the law (1.01)

6. traffic tickets (−1.58)

7. misdemeanor arrests (−.94)

8. felony arrests (−.80)

Performance criteria in which we find the most discrepancy between how police report they *should be* rated and how they report they *are* rated fall into two groups: criteria which should be more important (positive numbers) and criteria which should be less important (negative numbers).

Court presentation was the first criterion which police officers felt should be *more* important in their evaluations. More than one-half of the officers reported that this criterion should be given more importance than it is currently being given. The second criterion is discretion. Almost 45 percent of the officers indicated that discretion should be given more importance in their evaluations. Human relations skills and knowledge were the next criteria that officers felt should receive more importance. Equal enforcement of the law was the criterion with the next highest level of discrepancy.

The single measure that had the greatest discrepancy was the issuance of traffic tickets. This criterion had the largest number of officers (43%) reporting that it should receive less importance in their evaluations. Misdemeanor arrests had the next greatest discrepancy with almost 37 percent of the officers believing it should be less important as an indicator of job performance. In fact, 36 percent of the officers ranked felony arrests just below misdemeanor arrests as a criterion that should receive less importance. Our data demonstrate that police officers were likely to report discrepancies in evaluation criteria which are given more importance than criteria which are given less importance.

We analyzed the change scores by gender and ethnicity of officer, how long the individual has been a police officer, the district to which he or she is assigned, age, and level of education, to determine if any officer characteristic(s) accounted for any differences in the means. There were no significant relationships for any of the variables except ethnicity, which explained variation in the following: (1) misdemeanor arrests; (2) court presentation; (3) knowledge; and (4) discretion.

The data in Table 4-7 reveal that the Anglo officers (43%) were almost twice as likely as black (22%) or Hispanic officers (26%) to report that misdemeanor arrests should be given less importance in their evaluations. Black and Hispanic officers were

Table 4-7.
Police Officer Task Evaluations Mean Change Scores by Ethnicity

| | Mean Change | | |
Activity	Anglo	Black	Hispanic
Report Writing	.40	.15	.12
Appearance	.62	.49	.52
Judgment	1.01	.48	.48
Initiative	.98	.62	.40
Misdemeanor Arrests	-1.22	-.25	-.57
Traffic Tickets	-2.15	-.34	-.99
Felony Arrests	-1.05	-.16	-.59
Court Presentation	2.01	.04	.99
Knowledge	1.62	.35	.31
Human Relations Skills	1.25	.63	.70
Dependability	.65	.16	.25
Demeanor	.78	.33	.36
Ability to Get Along	.72	.33	.48
Courtesy	.64	.66	.62
No Complaints	-1.19	.33	-.05
Community Affairs	.27	-.23	-.09
No Personal Problems	.77	.19	.03
Equal Enforcement of the Law	1.18	.80	.65
Discretion	1.45	.31	.67
Use of Excessive Force for Image	-.04	.18	-.36

more likely to report that these arrests should be given greater importance than less importance. Black officers were significantly less likely (33%) than Anglo (53%) and Hispanic (53%) officers to report that court presentation should receive more importance than presently given in officer evaluations. Anglo officers are much more likely (52%) to report that knowledge should be given more importance in an evaluation than Hispanic officers (39%) or black officers (28%). Finally, black officers are less likely (24%) to believe that discretion should be a more important part of the evaluation than Hispanic officers (44%) or Anglo officers (50%).

Our look at the police officers' view of their own task evaluations revealed some interesting patterns. Overall, there were several significant change scores between the groups, as we have already noted. When mean changes within ethnic groups were viewed it is the Anglo officers who most often report dis-

Table 4-8.
Factor Loadings—Police Task Evaluations

Qualitative Measures				
1. Judgment	.73	1. Misdemeanor Arrests	.81
2. Initiative	.63	2. Traffic Tickets	.78
3. Knowledge	.71	3. Felony Arrests	.62
4. Human Relations	.76		
5. Dependability	.82		
6. Demeanor	.79		
7. Get Along	.83		
8. Courtesy	.78		
9. Discretion	.68		
64% Variance		23% Variance	

parate scores between what should be used for evaluations and what are used for evaluations. In both between-group and within-group analyses, there are criteria for evaluations which are clustered together. We noted that the crime-fighting activities appeared to be ranked close together at one end of the scale and the social service activities were grouped together toward the other end of the scale. This observation led us to take a closer look at the patterned observations of the criteria through a factor analysis.

We entered the scores of how officers think they should be evaluated into a factor analysis. Two clear factors emerged as shown in Table 4-8. This confirmed our suspicions (see Mastrofski, 1983; McIver and Parks, 1983; and Froemel, 1979). Using a very conservative rule for inclusion (.60), our analysis revealed a qualitative measures factor and a quantitative measures factor. The primary factor included nine qualitative measures including judgment, initiative, knowledge, human relations skills, dependability, demeanor, the ability to get along, courtesy and discretion. This factor alone explained 64 percent of the variance. The second factor included the quantitative measures of misdemeanor arrests, felony arrests and the issuance of traffic tickets. This factor explained 23 percent of the variance. Only two inter-item correlations were above .70: the ability to get along and courtesy (.83) were related, as were dependability and demeanor (.75).

The two strong factors which emerged from the factor analysis indicate the importance of the two types of measures which can be used for evaluations. On the one hand, the subjective or qualitative measures are the most important as indicators of good performance to the majority of the police officers. It is these types of measures which the officers believe are the most important criteria by which they should be evaluated. These criteria cluster together but do not measure the same thing. On the other hand, the objective or quantitative measures are seen as less important as measures of good performance and also cluster together while not measuring the same phenomenon.

The next step in the analysis was to create scales (both quantitative and qualitative) by adding the scores of the specific criteria and dividing by the number of items. We then determined if any particular police officer characteristic explained a significant amount of variance in the scores on the scales.

The first scale which measured the qualitative items received the highest mean scores. Officers had a mean score of 8.30 when asked about how they should be evaluated. When computed, they had a mean score of 7.48 on the scale that asked how they think they are evaluated. The mean difference is −.82, which infers that the qualitative measures are not given the importance that the officers believe they should be given.

The second scale which measured the quantitative items received mean scores significantly lower than the first scale. The officers' mean score on how the quantitative items should be used in evaluations was 5.42. On the quantitative scale, asking how the items are used in evaluations, the officers reported a mean score of 6.57. The mean difference for the quantitative scale is 1.15, meaning that the officers believe that the quantitative items are given more importance than they should be.

A COMPARISON OF CITIZEN AND
POLICE RANKINGS

The police task evaluation data which have just been discussed revealed several significant findings. First, they confirmed significant variation among the neighborhoods. Second, there exists variation among the police officers, and third, the major differences for all groups was between the qualitative and quantitative evaluation criteria.

A comparison of citizen and police rankings indicates that police officers do not necessarily place in the same order of priority those functions reported by members of the neighborhoods we studied. In order to receive a meritorious evaluation by residents, functions and tasks must be desired by members of the community and performed by the police in a similar system of priorities. In other words, police officers have ranked the various functions and tasks they perform, and will probably act accordingly. Placing priorities on police functions, and acting accordingly may be acceptable and even desired in some communities and neighborhoods. However, in other areas, the priority of functions and tasks performed by police may be undesirable and even unacceptable. For example, in Rolling Oaks, an officer will have to demonstrate courteous behavior, a good appearance, good human relations skills, and felony arrests. In the James Scott Housing Project, to be evaluated positively, officers will have to have a good appearance, show initiative and discretion and pay more attention to making arrests and issuing traffic tickets than they may think is important. In order to be successful in the 1960 Cuban immigrant neighborhood, police must demonstrate knowledge of procedures and laws, must make appropriate discretionary decisions and must be courteous. In the most recently formed neighborhood, the Cubans who immigrated in 1980 place the highest priorities on having no personal problems, a good court presentation and knowledge of procedures and laws. In Kendall, the mostly Anglo neighborhood, the residents report that police officers should be courteous, have a good demeanor toward the public, and make good judgments.

Overall, the residents in the two Cuban neighborhoods and Kendall have a closer agreement of policing priorities when compared to the police than do members of Rolling Oaks and the James Scott Housing Project. For whatever reasons, police and members of the black neighborhoods do not rank police tasks and functions as close as the Cuban and Anglo neighborhoods. This finding indicates that policing within the first three areas is more congruent and therefore less stressful between police officers and the public than policing in black neighborhoods. The interpretations of these findings and their implications will be explored in our final chapters.

5

Attitudes toward the Police and Policing

In this chapter, we outline the major findings on the five attitude scales which were derived from the factor analysis of the thirty attitude questions discussed in the methods section in Chapter 3. These scales represent five very different, yet interlocking attitude domains concerning the police officers' characteristics and behaviors. The first scale, *demeanor*, measures the perception of police characteristics such as courteousness, friendliness and respect for citizens. The next scale, *responsibility*, measures attitudes toward who has the most responsibility for the control of crime: the police or citizens. The last three scales measure attitudes toward different practices of the police: the use of *discretion* in applying the law, viewing *ethnic groups* differently, and active *patrol strategies*.

Our first concern is with the variability among neighborhoods on each of the five scales in relation to the variance within neighborhoods. In other words, we need to answer the question: is there more variance between neighborhoods than within neighborhoods? Second, we will examine significant differences in scale scores between males and females, as well as among ethnic and income groups (an indicator of social class). Social class and ethnicity, potentially the two major contaminating factors in our analysis, are controlled naturally by the research design through the selection of neighborhoods. Therefore, these variables do not need to be controlled statistically.

Our analysis demonstrates that there is almost no variation within neighborhoods on these two variables. However, to look closer at the overall effects of ethnicity and social class on the scale scores, we combine all neighborhood samples. In addition, we compare the neighborhoods with respect to the relative homogeneity of attitudes and values. Instead of using the absolute magnitudes of the standard deviations, we calculate coefficients of relative variation (CRV) which control for variation in the size of the means. The CRV is merely the standard deviation divided by the group mean, and can be interpreted as a standard deviation that is further standardized by the size of the mean. The lower the CRV, the greater the degree of cohesiveness within the group. This measure allows us to determine the relative cohesiveness (relative to the other groups) of opinions and values *within* each neighborhood on each of the scales. In addition, we can determine the relative cohesiveness of attitudes about each of the five scale constructs within the entire population of subjects.

Finally, we create neighborhood profiles and compare them to the scale scores of the police to determine the congruence between the expectations of the police and the citizens of the various neighborhoods (see Dunham and Alpert, 1988).

The data in Table 5-1 summarize the scores on the *Demeanor scale* for each of the neighborhood samples and for ethnic groups. Overall, the perception of police demeanor is slightly in the positive direction. As in all of the scales, a "one" signifies strong agreement with a positive statement about police demeanor. A "two" represents agreement, a "three" means undecided, a "four" signifies disagreement and a "five" represents strong disagreement. All of the means are less than three or in the agreement range. The 1960 Cuban immigrants perceive police demeanor the most positively. Kendall residents view police demeanor more positively than the remaining groups, but not nearly as much as the 1960 Cubans. The two black neighborhoods and the 1980 Cubans reported the most negative responses toward police demeanor. There is no significant difference between males and females on this scale. There are small but statistically significant differences between ethnic groups and perceptions of police demeanor. Anglos and Cubans gave

Table 5-1.
Scoring on the Demeanor Scale by Neighborhood
and Ethnicity

	Demeanor				
	Mean	S.D.	S.E.	N	CRV*
1. Rolling Oaks	2.88	.38	.05	49	.13
2. James Scott	2.82	.36	.05	43	.13
3. 1980 Cubans	2.88	.54	.08	49	.19
4. 1960 Cubans	2.46	.45	.06	50	.18
5. Kendall	2.64	.32	.05	.50	.12
6. Police	2.67	.29	.02	294	.11

Significance .000

Significantly Different Pairs (4 from 1, 2 and 3) (5
from 1 and 3) (6 from 1, 3 and 4)

1. Anglo	2.67	.35	.06	40
2. Black	2.84	.37	.04	87
3. Hispanic	2.66	.52	.05	104

Significance .022

Significantly Different Pairs (2 from 3)

*coefficient of relative variation ($V = \frac{S}{\bar{X}}$)

more positive evaluations of police demeanor than blacks. The relationship between family income and scores on the demeanor scale is significant (.053), but weak ($r = -.112$).

The significant main effect obtained from the analysis of variance indicates that the variance is more pronounced *between* neighborhoods than *within* neighborhoods.

The CRV analysis indicates that all of the neighborhoods are quite cohesive concerning attitudes about police demeanor, relative to the cohesiveness of groups on the other scales. In fact, each neighborhood had more internal cohesiveness on police demeanor than on any of the other attitude domains.

In summary, there is not a drastic amount of variance among groups on the demeanor scale. All of the groups report attitudes in a positive direction, and the 1960 Cubans and the Kendall residents hold the most positive perceptions of police de-

Table 5-2.
Scoring on the Responsibility Scale by Neighborhood
and Ethnicity

		Responsibility				
		Mean	S.D.	S.E.	N	CRV*
1.	Rolling Oaks	3.13	.88	.12	50	.28
2.	James Scott	3.26	.91	.14	45	.28
3.	1980 Cubans	2.52	.78	.11	50	.31
4.	1960 Cubans	2.40	.98	.14	50	.41
5.	Kendall	3.83	.56	.08	.50	.15
6.	Police	3.91	.65	.04	295	.17

Significance .000

Significantly Different Pairs (1 from 4 and 3) (2 from 4 and 3) (5 from 1, 2, 3 and 4) (6 from 1, 2, 3, and 4)

1.	Anglo		3.91	.50	.08	40
2.	Black		3.20	.89	.09	90
3.	Hispanic		2.50	.86	.08	105

Significance .000

Significantly Different Pairs (3 from 1 and 2) (2 from 1)

*coefficient of relative variation ($V = \frac{S}{X}$)

meanor. There is not any evidence here for a need to develop specific neighborhood strategies concerning police demeanor.

The data in Table 5-2 summarize the scores on the *Responsibility scale*. There are clear differences among neighborhoods on whether the major responsibility for controlling crime lies with the police. The two Cuban groups agree with this notion while all of the other groups disagree. Further, of those groups that disagree, the Kendall residents report the strongest disagreement. The Kendall residents not only report the strongest disagreement, but also have the highest level of consensus as indicated by a comparison of the CRVs. In contrast, the two Cuban groups are the only groups agreeing that the police are solely responsible for crime control, and they have the lowest level of consensus.

There is not significant difference between males and females on this scale, and its relationship with family income is non-significant. The breakdown on the three ethnic groups indicates that the Cubans were the only ones to agree with the idea that the major responsibility for crime control rests with the police. All others disagreed. The Anglo respondents reported the strongest disagreement. With the exception of the Kendall residents, each neighborhood group reported lower levels of consensus on the responsibility scale when compared to the other four scales.

The data in Table 5-3 summarize the scores on the *Discretion scale* for each of the samples. The general sentiment among all groups is that police *should* use considerable discretion when applying procedural safeguards and other police procedures in the different neighborhoods. The respondents in both of the Cuban neighborhoods gave the strongest approval for the use of discretion, and the residents of Rolling Oaks gave the weakest level of approval. Even these lower scoring groups, however, approve of the use of discretion, it is just that they approve of it less emphatically than the other groups. Due to the low reliability coefficients of this scale for two of our neighborhoods (James Scott and the 1980 Cuban immigrants), interpretation of these findings is only suggestive and tentative and should not be extended to these two neighborhoods.

As in the demeanor and responsibility scales, gender was not a significant factor. Family income was significantly related to scores on this scale (.019), but the relationship is very weak ($r = .143$). When combining all groups, the blacks reported the weakest level of approval for the use of discretion when compared to Anglos and Latins.

In sum, there is more overall agreement in attitudes toward police use of discretion than for any of the other scales. The two Cuban groups report the strongest agreement, while residents of Rolling Oaks showed the weakest agreement. Blacks, in general, showed the weakest level of agreement. Analysis of

Table 5-3.
Scoring on the Discretion Scale by Neighborhood
and Ethnicity

		Discretion				
		Mean	S.D.	S.E.	N	CRV*
1.	Rolling Oaks	2.71	.73	.11	48	.27
2.	James Scott	2.55	.67	.11	39	.26
3.	1980 Cubans	2.03	.52	.07	49	.26
4.	1960 Cubans	1.86	.61	.09	50	.33
5.	Kendall	2.22	.66	.09	50	.30
6.	Police	2.70	.83	.05	295	.31

Significance .000

Significantly Different Pairs (1 frokm 4 and 3) (2 from 4 and 3) (5 from 1, 2, 3 and 4) (6 from 1, 2, 3, and 4)

		Mean	S.D.	S.E.	N	
1.	Anglo	2.21	.71	.11	40	
2.	Black	2.63	.69	.08	82	
3.	Hispanic	1.96	.56	.05	104	

Significance .000

Significantly Different Pairs (2 from 1 and 3)

*coefficient of relative variation ($V = \frac{S}{X}$)

the CRVs indicates a moderate level of consensus within groups that is quite evenly distributed among the groups.

The data in Table 5-4 summarize the scores for the *Ethnic Suspicion scale*. Generally, all of the study groups except one disapproved of the notion that some ethnic groups need to be watched more closely for criminal activity than others. The one exception is the James Scott project. The mean score for this group indicates that these respondents either agreed or were undecided about the need to watch some ethnic groups more closely than others. The residents of the 1960 Cuban neighbor-

Table 5-4.
Scoring on the Ethnic Scale by Neighborhood and Ethnicity

		Ethnic				
		Mean	S.D.	S.E.	N	CRV*
1.	Rolling Oaks	3.70	.71	.10	50	.19
2.	James Scott	2.94	.61	.09	43	.21
3.	1980 Cubans	3.33	.79	.11	50	.24
4.	1960 Cubans	3.93	.61	.09	50	.16
5.	Kendall	3.75	.75	.11	50	.20
6.	Police	3.81	.61	.04	296	.16

Significance   .03

Significantly Different Pairs (2 from 1, 4 and 5) (3 from 5) (6 from 2 and 3)

1.	Anglo	3.74	.75	.12	40
2.	Black	3.35	.75	.08	88
3.	Hispanic	3.60	.78	.08	105

Significance   .000

Significantly Different Pairs (1 from 2)

*coefficient of relative variation ($V = \frac{S}{\bar{X}}$)

hood responded with the strongest disagreement of ethnic suspicion. There is no significant difference between males and females on this scale and a significant (.003) but weak relationship with family income ($r = .191$). Anglos are significantly stronger in disagreement with this idea than blacks, while Cubans score in between the Anglos and the blacks.

Analysis of CRVs shows a high level of consensus within neighborhoods on the ethnic suspicion scale when compared to responses of the other scales. In addition, consensus levels are fairly evenly distributed across the groups.

There exists a general disagreement with the idea that ethnic

Table 5-5.
Scoring on the Patrol Scale by Neighborhood and Ethnicity

		Patrol				
		Mean	S.D.	S.E.	N	CRV*
1.	Rolling Oaks	3.12	.79	.11	50	.25
2.	James Scott	3.02	.74	.11	44	.25
3.	1980 Cubans	2.55	.74	.11	50	.35
4.	1960 Cubans	2.16	.97	.14	50	.45
5.	Kendall	2.96	1.01	.14	49	.34
6.	Police	2.54	.84	.05	295	.33

Significance .000
Significantly Different Pairs (4 from 1, 2 and 5)
(3 from 1) (6 from 1, 2, and 5)

1.	Anglo			2.99	1.02	.16	39
2.	Black			3.10	.73	.08	89
3.	Latin			2.36	.95	.09	105

Significance .000

Significantly Different Pairs (3 from 1 and 2)

*coefficient of relative variation ($V = \frac{s}{\bar{x}}$)

suspicion is justified, except for the residents of the James Scott housing project, who generally agree. The 1960 Cubans disagree more than the residents of other neighborhoods, while Anglos disagree more strongly than any other ethnic group.

In Table 5-5 we summarize the scores on the scale testing for agreement or disagreement with *active patrol strategies*. There is considerable variation among groups concerning agreement with these strategies. In fact, there is more variation among groups on this scale than on any of the other four scales. This scale also has the lowest level of consensus within neighborhoods, as demonstrated by the CRV analysis. The first wave of Cuban entrants (1960) approve of active patrol strategies more than any other group. The 1980 Cuban entrants also approve of these strategies, but not as strongly as their earlier cohort. Finally, Kendall residents reported weak agreement with active patrol strategies, while Rolling Oaks and James Scott disagree with these strategies. There are no significant gender effects. Family income is significantly related to scores on this scale (.040), but the relationship is weak (r = .120). When combining all the samples together, it is the Cubans who stand out as different from the other ethnic groups. They agree that active patrol strategies are appropriate, while blacks and Anglos have an average near the undecided category. However, this does not mean that residents do not have opinions on active patrol strategies.

Analysis of the CRVs indicates that there is considerable disagreement within groups on this procedure for the black neighborhoods and Kendall residents. For example, residents of the 1960 Cuban neighborhood showed the highest level of agreement with active patrol strategies, but they had considerable disagreement within the group. This is demonstrated by the CRV of .45, which is the highest CRV for any neighborhood on any scale.

Neighborhood Profiles

It is instructive to assess the level of consensus for each neighborhood across the five scales and to indicate the general level of consensus within each neighborhood. Put in the form of a question, do certain neighborhoods have a greater degree of agreement on their general feelings about the police and police practices? The 1960 Cubans had the highest average CRV (.31) indicating the weakest level of overall consensus. Remember, they also had the most extreme attitudes on many of the police practices. They showed fairly strong consensus on the demeanor and ethnic scales, but the weakest levels of consensus on the three remaining scales. Kendall residents reached a very high level of consensus on three of the scales (demeanor, responsibility and ethnic), but showed some disagreement on the discretion and patrol scales. Residents of both the black neighborhoods, Rolling Oaks and James Scott, had fairly even levels of consensus across the scales. The 1980 Cubans were moderate in their levels of consensus across all five scales when compared to the other four neighborhoods.

Next, a profile of the attitudes prevalent in each neighborhood will be compared to the attitudes of the police. These profiles are far from complete, but they include information on many relevant police practices.

1. *Rolling Oaks*: The police held significantly different attitudes on three of the five scales when compared to the attitudes prevalent in this neighborhood. The police perceived their demeanor to be more positive than the slightly positive rankings of these residents, which was the weakest level of approval in any of the neighborhoods. The police disagreed more strongly than did these residents with the placement of crime control on the police. More significantly, the police agreed with the appropriateness of active patrol strategies in contrast to the residents' general disagreement.

2. *James Scott*: There are significant differences between the attitudes of the police and these residents on three of the scales. The police disagreed more strongly than these residents that the primary responsibility for crime control rests with the police. A significant disagreement occurs over the idea that certain ethnic groups need to be watched more closely than others. Interestingly, the police generally disagreed with this idea, while James Scott residents were the only ones to agree. In addition, the police differed significantly with these citizens over the appropriateness of active patrol strategies. The police generally agreed, while the residents disagreed with these strategies.

3. *1980 Cuban Immigrants*: The police scores were significantly different from the scores of these residents on four of the five scales. The police viewed police demeanor more positively than these residents, and they disagreed with the idea that the major responsibility for crime control rests with the police, while residents agreed with the idea. An interesting difference here is that the police reported only weak agreement with the appropriateness of using discretion in applying procedural safeguards, while these residents showed the strongest agreement of any of the neighborhoods. The police reported stronger disagreement with the appropriateness of ethnic suspicion than the residents, who showed only weak disagreement.

4. *1960 Cuban Immigrants*: The police differed significantly with these residents on three of the scales. In this neighborhood, the residents viewed police demeanor more positively than the police themselves. Similarly, the residents showed stronger approval of the appropriateness of police discretion in applying procedural safe-

guards than did the police. In both of these comparisons, the residents are in agreement with the attitudes of police officers, but report more extreme attitudes. The one real disagreement between the police and the residents of this neighborhood is over who should shoulder the major responsibility for crime control. The police disagree with the citizens who think it is mainly a police responsibility.

5. *Kendall*: The attitudes of the police were the most congruent with the attitudes of these residents. The police differed significantly on only two of the scales, and these differences were minor. The police were a little weaker than Kendall residents on their approval of the use of discretion in applying procedural safeguards. In addition, the police were a little stronger than these residents on their approval of active patrol strategies. This group of residents had the strongest acceptance of community involvement with crime control than in any of the other neighborhoods.

SUMMARY

The data collected from these attitude scales have demonstrated distinct differences among our ethnic groups. Further, comparisons of these different neighborhood profiles with the attitudes of the police indicate that the police have views quite congruent with some neighborhoods and quite incongruent with others. It appears that the Hispanic groups, who display support for the police in general, also report high levels of agreement with specific forms of policing portrayed by our measures, but do not support the use of ethnic distinctions in directing police activities. One of the few areas in which the black respondents differed substantially from the Anglos and Hispanics, was in showing disapproval of active patrol strategies. It is also interesting that, given the recent history of black rioting in response to police actions, those black citizens were not as negative as we expected. Perhaps these social disturbances did not symbolize a generalized disenchantment with the police, but reflected a mood of political and social disenchantment.

This chapter has focused upon the description of the five attitudinal scales concerning police and policing. Implications of these findings are discussed in the concluding chapter. The following chapter will focus upon attitudes toward the criminal justice system and social institutions in general, to provide a context for understanding attitudes toward the police.

6

Attitudes toward the Police and Other Social Institutions

Now that we have discussed neighborhood differences in evaluating the importance of various police tasks, and in reporting agreement or disagreement with different police strategies and procedures, we need to take a closer look at general evaluations of the police. It is these general assessments of the police which help us characterize the neighborhood context in which the police must operate.

Social researchers and public policy analysts have had a long-standing interest in citizens' attitudes toward the police. In light of the number of studies assessing citizens' attitudes toward the police, it is interesting that almost without exception these studies have assessed attitudes toward the police in a social vacuum (Decker, 1981; Scaglion and Condon, 1980; White and Menke, 1978; Alpert and Hicks, 1977; Casper, 1972; for an exception, see Alpert and Green, 1977). Research on police generally fails to consider the larger attitude complex that is the foundation on which the more specific attitudes are based.

It is the purpose of this chapter to examine neighborhood variations in attitudes toward the police within the context of one's more comprehensive attitude complex, including attitudes toward the criminal justice system and toward social institutions in general. We attempt to identify the aspects of the larger contextual environment that may help in forming interpretations of citizens' attitudes toward the police as they aggregate in each neighborhood context.

This multi-level analysis, as applied to attitudinal research, can be empirically examined only if due attention is paid to significant features of a more comprehensive set of attitudes. As Mandel (1983) spoke of local and global roles in relation to the social network, we refer to local and global attitudes in relation to social institutions. The first attitude is a simplification of the second, and the first (more focused) attitude is nested in the second (more complex) attitude. An important part of this analysis is to examine the correspondence among the levels to assist in interpreting neighborhood differences in attitudes toward the police.

Albrecht and Green (1977) demonstrate that attitudes toward the police are intimately interwoven into the fabric of the more general attitude complex. They found a correspondence between negative attitudes toward the police and professionals in the court system. Further, they found a significant, but weaker correspondence between negative attitudes toward the police and general feelings of political alienation and powerlessness.

Lipset and Schneider (1983) report that people tend to distrust and have little confidence in large and powerful institutions because they are so removed from our influence and experience. In comparison, however, local representatives of these same institutions are more trusted by the same subjects surveyed. They note: "Whenever surveys have dealt with different size levels of the same institution, they have found greater hostility to the big or large versions than to the smaller ones" (Lipset and Schneider, 1983:81).

It is clear that the meaning of one's attitude toward the police varies according to the mind-set of the subject. For example, one subject may have a very negative attitude toward the police, but further inspection may reveal that this subject holds very negative attitudes about most major institutions in our society. The negative attitude toward the police, in the larger context, seems to indicate that this is just a very negative person who does not hold any special disdain for the police. Another subject, who also holds a very negative attitude toward the police, may indicate generally a very favorable attitude toward most of society's institutions. Clearly, the meaning of the negative attitudes toward the police held by these two subjects is different, but may be masked if analyzed independently of other attitudes. A second subject may feel generally positive about social institutions, but for some reason display some uncharacteristically negative attitudes toward the police. The second subject should be of greater concern to the police than the first. Conversely, it is possible for a subject to hold consistently negative attitudes toward most of our social institutions and yet be favorably disposed when it comes to the police. Further, a subject may display quite favorable attitudes toward the police that simply may reflect his/her general confidence and trust in most of society's social institutions. Of course, there are other contexts within which it is possible to analyze attitudes toward the police. The context of the larger criminal justice system (prosecutors, judges and defense attorneys), for example, can enhance our understanding of attitudes toward the police. In the present chapter, we incorporate both of these levels (attitudes toward social institutions in general and toward the criminal justice system) as important contextual variables for understanding the significance of reported attitudes toward the police.

Our measures of attitudes toward components of the criminal justice system will be used to develop scales for the first two levels of analysis (the police and the criminal justice system). The scale on attitudes toward the police is used for the first level. The four criminal justice scales including the prosecutors, judges, defense attorneys and the police are averaged to form a new scale for the criminal justice system in general. We left the police in the criminal justice scale to make comparisons more conservative between the first two levels. Finally, we use the confidence and trust scales to represent attitudes toward major social institutions.

For each individual subject, we computed the scores on the three scales into three categories: positive, neutral and negative. We also computed change scores between the three levels of analysis. The percentage of subjects falling into the positive, neutral and negative categories for each of our samples at the three levels of analysis is listed in Table 6-1. At the institutional level, the figures for both competence and trust are shown.

Table 6-1.
Percentage of Each Sample Which Is Positive, Neutral or Negative toward the Police, Justice System and the Overall Social System

| | Social System | | | | | | Justice System | | | Police | | |
| | Competence | | | Trust | | | | | | | | |
	Pos	Neu	Neg	Pos	Neu	Neg	Pos	Neu	Neg	Pos	Neu	Neg
Students	48%	41%	11%	36%	54%	11%	53%	34%	13%	50%	40%	10%
Polic	14%	68%	18%	14%	64%	22%	27%	60%	14%	63%	31%	6%
Rolling Oaks	10%	80%	10%	6%	80%	14%	16%	80%	4%	22%	64%	14%
James Scott	20%	40%	40%	26%	38%	36%	12%	68%	20%	32%	46%	22%
1960 Cubans	60%	24%	16%	62%	26%	12%	80%	14%	6%	90%	8%	2%
1980 Cubans	54%	24%	22%	48%	28%	24%	58%	14%	28%	60%	16%	24%
Kendall	42%	42%	16%	30%	64%	6%	48%	36%	16%	72%	22%	6%
Total	35%	49%	16%	29%	55%	16%	43%	43%	14%	55%	35%	10%
N	352	490	155	289	550	158	426	435	136	552	347	98

Looking at all groups together, we find a linear relationship when moving from the more general level of social institutions to the specific level (police). For example, 35 percent (29 percent for trust) reported positive scores at the societal level, 43 percent at the justice system level, and 55 percent at the police level. Attitudes, therefore, become more positive as we move from the general level of social institutions to the specific level of police. The same relationship, except in reverse, is found for negative attitudes. For example, at the social system level, 16 percent reported negative attitudes, 14 percent reported scores at the justice system level, and only 10 percent had negative attitudes toward the police.

Taking each sample separately *students* showed very little variation in percentage of positive or negative responses across the three levels. This indicates that they evaluate the police about the same as they evaluate our major social institutions and the criminal justice system.

Police become more positive as they move from the social system level to the specific domain of police. They rank themselves extremely high when compared to the other two levels of our society.

Rolling Oaks residents report the fewest positive responses in each of the three levels. These respondents become more positive as they move from the general attitude domain of social institutions to the specific attitude toward police. This group reports the highest percentage of neutral responses in each of the categories.

The attitudes of the *James Scott* residents deviate from linearity in that they have fewer positive responses toward the justice system than the other two levels. These residents evaluate the police higher than the other two levels. In each of the levels, they report more negative responses with the exception of the 1980 Cuban entrants.

1960 Cuban Entrants report more positive attitudes on all three levels than any other group, and very few negative responses. These respondents become more positive as they move from the general social system to the police.

1980 Cuban Entrants are generally positive toward all three levels and become more positive as they move from the general to the specific attitude toward police. However, these respondents report the greatest number of negative responses when evaluating the justice system and the police.

Kendall residents reflect middle range attitudes toward all three levels. As they move from the general societal level to the police, they report increasingly positive attitudes.

To examine further attitudes toward the police in the context of attitudes toward the larger social system, we computed change scores depicting the differences between attitudes toward each of the levels. To compare attitudes at each level, we examine change scores for each sample. The data in Table 6-2 summarize the differences between attitudes toward the social system level (competence) and the justice system level. These indicate that overall, 47 percent of our samples hold different attitudes when comparing the two levels. Twenty-nine percent hold more positive attitudes toward the justice system than toward the social system in general, while only 18 percent have more negative attitudes toward the justice system. Kendall residents were more likely than any other group to be more positive toward the criminal justice system (38%), while the Marielitos had the lowest percentage in the "more positive" category (22%). The Kendall sample also had the highest percentage of responses in the "more negative" category (30%). The 1960 Cuban immigrants had the fewest in the "more negative" category (4%). Students, Marielitos, and Kendall residents each had about equal percentages in the two change categories ("more negative" or "more positive"), indicating no overall trend in these samples weighted in either direction ("more negative" or "more positive"). The police, Rolling Oaks and James Scott residents reported more than double the percentage in the "more positive" category as in the "more negative" category, indicating more positive attitudes toward the justice system when compared to the social system in general. The 1960 Cuban immigrants had nearly eight times the percentage of residents falling in the "more positive" category than in the "more negative" category. The differences at this level were not significant for gender, but were significantly different for ethnic groups. These data are reported in Table 6-3. A greater percentage of blacks fell into the

Table 6-2.
Percentage of Each Sample with Different Attitudes toward the Justice System Than toward the Social System in General

	More Negative	No Difference	More Positive
Students	21%	51%	28%
Police	15%	52%	32%
Rolling Oaks	10%	70%	20%
James Scott	18%	48%	34%
1980 Cubans	22%	56%	22%
1960 Cubans	4%	66%	30%
Kendall	30%	32%	38%
Total	18%	52%	29%
N	183	521	293

Significance Level = .0029

"more negative" category than Anglos and hispanics, while a greater percentage of Anglos were in the "more positive" group.

The data in Table 6-4 summarize the percentage of each sample who are more negative and more positive toward the police than toward the overall criminal justice system. Examining all samples together, we find that there are more than twice as many subjects in the "more positive" category than in the "more negative" category. Two-thirds of the subjects reported no difference in attitudes toward the police when compared to the

Table 6-3.
Percentage of Each Ethnic Group with Different Attitudes toward the Justice System Than toward the Social System in General

	More Negative	No Difference	More Positive
Anglo	17%	50%	33%
Black	22%	49%	29%
Hispanic	15%	59%	27%
Other*	31%	40%	21%
Total	18%	50%	33%
N	179	512	289

Significance Level = .028

*The other category is not discussed due to an extremely low N.

Table 6-4.
Percentage of Each Sample with Different Attitudes toward the Police Than toward the Justice System in General

	More Negative	No Difference	More Positive
Student	15%	72%	13%
Police	4%	53%	44%
Rolling Oaks	16%	72%	12%
James Scott	12%	60%	28%
1980 Cubans	4%	88%	8%
1960 Cubans	0%	88%	12%
Kendall	6%	64%	30%
Total	10%	67%	23%
N	99	666	232

Significance Level = .0000

Table 6-5.
Percentage of Males and Females with Different Attitudes toward
the Police Than toward the Justice System in General

		More Negative	No Difference	More Positive
Positive				
Male		7%	62%	29%
Female		12%	74%	14%
	Total	10%	67%	23%
	N	98	658	227

Significance Level = .0000

justice system. The group with the greatest number having different attitudes was the police. Police officers are overwhelmingly more positive toward themselves than toward others in the criminal justice system (44%). Both Cuban groups had the highest percentage in the "no difference" group (88%), in part because they rated all professionals in the criminal justice system very high. When comparing the "more positive" to the "more negative" categories, students and residents of Rolling Oaks had about equal numbers in each group. James Scott residents and the Marielitos had about twice as many in the "more positive" category than in the "more negative" category, and the police, Kendall residents and the 1960 Cubans each had an even greater imbalance in favor of "more positive" attitudes toward the police than toward the criminal justice system as a whole.

Data in Table 6-5 indicate that the differences at this level (justice system–police) are significant for both gender and ethnicity. Twice as many males as females are more positive toward the police than toward the criminal justice system generally, and nearly twice as many females as males are more negative toward the police. The data in Table 6-6 reveal that Anglos are nearly twice as likely to be in the "more positive" category than blacks and Hispanics, while blacks are two to three times more likely to be in the "more negative" category.

Data comparing attitudes toward the police with attitudes

Table 6-6.
Percentage of Ethnic Groups with Different Attitudes toward the
Police and the Justice System in General

	More Negative	No Difference	More Positive
Anglo	5%	60%	35%
Black	16%	68%	16%
Hispanic	8%	73%	20%
Other	0%	72%	28%
Total	10%	67%	23%
N	96	656	228

Significance Level = .0000

toward major social institutions in general are presented in Table 6-7. When combining all samples, 55 percent had different attitudes about the police than they had about the social system in general. Thirty-nine percent of all the subjects were more positive about the police than about the social system in general. Only 16 percent of the group was more negative about the police than the general system. Again, the police sample had the most responses in the "more positive" category (62%), and very few in the "more negative" category (9%). Kendall and James Scott residents also had high percentages in the "more positive" category (48% and 44% respectively).

The 1960 Cubans and the police had very low percentages of responses in the "more negative category" (10% and 9% respectively). All of the samples had more subjects who were more positive toward the police than more negative. Students and Marielitos had about equal percentages in the "more positive" and "more negative" categories, while the 1960 Cubans, police and Kendall residents had more than double the percentage of responses in the "more positive" category than in the "more negative" category.

As reported in Table 6-8 and 6-9, differences between these two levels (social system–police) are significantly different for both gender and ethnicity. Males are more likely to be in the

Table 6-7.
Percentage of Each Sample with Different Attitudes toward the
Police and the Social System in General

	More Negative	No Difference	More Positive
Students	22%	51%	26%
Police	9%	29%	62%
Rolling Oaks	18%	58%	24%
James Scott	20%	36%	44%
1980 Cubans	20%	58%	22%
1960 Cubans	0%	64%	36%
Kendall	16%	36%	48%
Total	16%	45%	39%
N	164	388	388

Significance Level = .0000

"more positive" toward police category and less likely to be in
the "more negative" category than females. Anglos had the
highest percentage of responses in the "more positive" category and the lowest percentage in the "more negative" category.

A final analysis of attitudes toward the police in the context

Table 6-8.
Percentage of Males and Females with Different Attitudes toward
the Police Than toward the Social System in General

	More Negative	No Difference	More Positive
Male	15%	41%	45%
Female	19%	51%	30%
Total	16%	45%	39%
N	161	439	383

Significance Level = .0000

Table 6-9.
Percentage of Each Ethnic Group with Different Attitudes toward
the Police Than toward the Social System in General

		More Negative	No Difference	More Positive
Anglo		8%	39%	53%
Black		25%	46%	29%
Hispanic		15%	49%	37%
Other		17%	52%	31%
	Total	16%	45%	39%
	N	160	438	382

Significance Level = .0000

of attitudes toward other social institutions was designed to
identify and to describe extreme groups in the three-levels
analysis. For example, are there any subjects who are extremely negative about the social system in general and yet
positive toward the police, or vice versa? If so, who are they
and what are their characteristics?

The information presented in Table 6-10 indicates that out of
all those negative toward the police (N = 98 or less than 10%
of entire study sample), 41 percent are positive toward the social system in general. Only 18 percent of those negative toward
the police are also negative about the entire social system. Out
of the 552 subjects who are positive toward the police (55% of
the entire study sample), 13 percent are negative toward the
social system in general. The two groups with conflicting attitudes about the two levels (police and the social system) are:
(1) people generally positive about social institutions, yet negative about the police, and (2) people generally negative about
social institutions but positive toward the police.

The data presented in Table 6-11 parallel the same analysis
in Table 6-10, except that we compare attitudes toward the police with attitudes toward the criminal justice system instead of
with social institutions in general. The data summarized in Table 6-11 reveal that most of those reporting negative attitudes

Table 6-10.
Percentage of Subjects with Conflicting Attitudes about the Police
and Social System in General

SOCIAL SYSTEM	POLICE		
	Positive	Neutral	Negative
Positive	41%	24%	41%
Neutral	46%	57%	41%
Negative	13%	18%	18%
	552	347	98

Significance Level = .0000

toward the police are also negative about the whole criminal justice system (65%). Only 2 percent of those negative about the police are also positive about the entire criminal justice system. At the other end of the scale, we find the 6 percent of those positive about the police are negative about the criminal justice system in general. These subjects apparently hold some special regard for the police while evaluating the entire criminal justice system negatively.

Our next step is to describe the four groups with conflicting attitudes toward the police and the other two levels (the criminal justice system and social institutions in general):

1. Subjects generally positive toward social institutions, but negative toward the police
2. Subjects generally negative toward social institutions, but positive toward the police
3. Subjects positive toward the criminal justice system, but negative toward the police
4. Subjects negative toward the criminal justice system, but positive toward the police

Table 6-11.
Percentage of Subjects with Conflicting Attitudes about the Police and the Justice System

	POLICE		
JUSTICE SYSTEM	Positive	Neutral	Negative
Positive	65%	19%	2%
Neutral	29%	70%	33%
Negative	6%	11%	65%
	552	347	98

Significance Level = .0000

The third category, positive about the criminal justice system, but negative about the police, includes only two subjects. Since this example of conflicting attitudes almost never happens, it will be dropped from any further analysis.

The data in Table 6-12 summarize information about each of the three remaining groups, those with conflicting attitudes between levels.

Positive Toward Social System–Negative Toward Police. Students are strongly over-represented in this group, while the police and the 1960 Cuban immigrants are strongly under-represented. Rolling Oaks residents are slightly under-represented, while the James Scott residents and the 1980 Cuban immigrants are slightly over-represented. Males are under-represented in this group and females are over-represented. Anglos are strongly over-represented and blacks strongly under-represented. Finally, both groups of Cubans are slightly under-represented. Respondents who fit into this group are significantly older than the group average (this excludes students; see note at bottom of Table 6-12).

Table 6-12.
Description of Extreme Groups in the Three Level Analysis

	Sample Statistics	Pos.- Social System Neg.- Police	Neg.- Social System Pos.- Police	Neg.- Social System Pos.- Police
Students	45%	63%	27%	40%
Police	30%	15%	43%	36%
Rolling Oaks	5%	3%	3%	–
James Scott	5%	8%	8%	3%
1980 Latins	5%	8%	6%	3%
1960 Latins	5%	–	6%	3%
Kendall	5%	5%	8%	15%
	N=997	(N=40)	(N=73)	(N=33)

	Sample Statistics	Pos.- Social System Neg.- Police	Neg.- Social System Pos.- Police	Neg.- Social System Pos.- Police
Male	59%	48%	68%	61%
Female	41%	52%	32%	39%
	N=997	(N=40)	(N=73)	(N=53)
Anglo	32%	16%	36%	42%
Black	34%	55%	35%	30%
Hispanic	31%	24%	27%	24%
Other	3%	5%	1%	3%
Mean Age*	37.32	41.27	37.90	41.85

*Age is missing on all students.
Therefore, age refers to all groups except students.

To summarize, students, and to a lesser degree James Scott residents and Marielitos, make up this group that holds special disdain for the police. In addition to these groups, it is the females and blacks who are most likely to have these attitudes.

Negative Toward the Social System–Positive Toward the Police. Students are strongly under-represented in this category and Rolling Oaks residents are slightly under-represented. The police are strongly over-represented in this group and James Scott and Kendall residents are slightly over-represented. Males are more likely than females to be negative toward the social system and positive toward the police. Ethnicity is significant: Anglos are slightly over-represented and blacks are slightly under-represented. This group consists of the youngest subjects of those with conflicting attitudes (excluding students; see note at bottom of Table 6-12).

Police, and to a lesser degree James Scott and Kendall residents, make up this category of subjects that are generally negative about social institutions, yet have special regard for the police. In addition to these groups, males and Anglos are the most likely to report these attitudes.

Negative Toward the Justice System–Positive Toward the Police. Kendall residents are strongly over-represented and the police are moderately over-represented in the group that evaluates the criminal justice system negatively but reports positive attitudes toward the police. Rolling Oaks residents and the students are moderately under-represented, while James Scott residents and the two Latin groups are slightly under-represented. Gender is not significant, but Anglos are more likely to be in this group, while blacks and Cubans are under-represented. Subjects in this group are older than the average.

SUMMARY

It is apparent from our analyses of attitudes toward three levels of the social structure that attitudes directed toward each level are divergent, and vary by neighborhood. Further, it is clear that attitudes toward the different levels are interrelated in several ways. First, attitudes toward one level (i.e., police) may be nested in attitudes toward a more general level (i.e., the justice system). Second, attitudes toward a more general level (i.e., social institutions in general) may indicate a generally positive or generally negative orientation that provides the basis for interpreting the attitudes toward a more specific level (i.e., the police).

If researchers fail to give due attention to significant features of the larger attitude complex, interpretations of the attitudes will be out of context and possibly biased. This study is just a beginning in sorting out the more general attitude complex and its relationship to attitudes toward the police. However, we were able to identify some of the aspects of the larger attitude complex that are important in interpreting attitudes toward the police and policing. Further research should develop standard measures and procedures to examine the interrelationshps more specifically.

In the samples we studied, the data confirm for the police Lipset and Schneider's (1983) finding that people have more positive attitudes concerning local representatives of an institution when compared to the levels that are more removed. The police, being the most frequently confronted professionals in the criminal justice system, enjoy the highest levels of approval.

Lipset and Schneider (1983:125) conclude that each institution has its own social and political bases of support. Patterns of support for institutions across the population tend to be specific and distinct for each institution. Lipset and Schneider report that shifts in confidence over time tend to be broad, general and responsive to events in the external environment, but that there is no specific location of "confidence" per se. Our findings from Miami are contrary to this conclusion. Cubans as a group report much stronger levels of support *at all three levels:* the police, the criminal justice system and social institutions in general. Even though the Cubans as a group are extremely supportive of the police and serve as their basis of support in Miami, it is important to interpret this support in the context of their generally positive orientation toward all three levels.

When focusing on negative attitudes toward the police, we found that they are firmly nested in negative attitudes about the criminal justice system as a whole. However, they do not correspond very closely to negative attitudes concerning social institutions in general. This conclusion points to the necessity of interpreting negative attitudes toward the police in the context of attitudes toward the criminal justice system.

7

Conclusions: Police Task Evaluations

Our research has looked at some major issues that are currently of great interest to police managers and municipal leaders. While it is inappropriate to suggest that all police departments will improve their work products or image in the community by following our suggestions, there are a number of findings which merit a cautious interpretation. We will proceed by discussing first our police task evaluations, moving to a discussion of the attitudes concerning police policies and practices, and finally to attitudes toward the police in the context of other social institutions. We will follow this discussion of our conclusions with a model of policing which includes an interaction between members of the community and the police. Our interactive model calls for policing strategies that integrate formal procedures and practices of the police (the formal control system) with the informal social control system operating within the various neighborhoods. The discussion of our conclusions and of the subsequent policy implications focus on the interaction between these two levels of the social control system.

POLICE TASK EVALUATIONS

There has been a long-standing belief among police officers that they are evaluated by criteria different from those by which they think are appropriate. The present research supports that belief and, in addition, found that residents in our five areas disagree on which police tasks should be given the highest priority. Assigning a priority system for police tasks is one indicator of the basic informal control structure in a neighborhood. These findings reinforce the notion that police administrators should structure their formal control system as consistently as possible with the informal control system operating with the neighborhoods. This can be accomplished by determining what tasks community members as well as their officers believe are the most important, and use this information to determine what criteria should be used to evaluate their officers.

In any organization it is important that the supervisors and the front-line workers understand each other, the rules under which they operate, and the desires of the consumers concerning their work products. Police work is no exception to this rule, and perhaps in this context such an information exchange is more important than in many other service-delivery professions. Unfortunately, there are serious problems relating to law enforcement and public safety that impede some information flow between the police and the community. The concern for public safety and efficient law enforcement is necessary, as is the need for a smooth-running organization that has strong internal and external relations.

Traditional police-community relations programs have stressed the need for town meetings and information transfer, but in practice, this has often been done in a haphazard fashion without clear benefits for either the police or community members. On both sides, good intentions have been present, but sufficient information exchange and action have both been lacking. The areas that need strengthening have not been identified correctly and the methods used to secure mutual understanding have not been effective. While there are many methods that can be used to evaluate the performance of police officers, without empirical evidence, it is difficult to determine if one method is better than another.

Policing can be simplified into two distinct types of work products: law enforcement and service delivery. These prod-

Figure 7-1.
Interaction between Formal and Informal Control Systems

ucts can be assessed by quantitative and qualitative measures. How police officers are assessed and how they should be assessed is the specific issue which leads to many misconceptions both on the part of police officers and members of the community. Our research has identified this particular division of work products as the basis for differences among police, and between police and the community.

There are several basic approaches which must be followed if police evaluations are to receive the support of officers and community members, which follow an interactive model (see Figure 7-1). First, the criteria used to evaluate police officers must be consistent with the police mission and how officers are trained to perform. Second, police officers must agree upon the criteria to be used, and how they are to be measured. Third, the community members served by the police must support the methods used to evaluate police, as these evaluations will shape the style of policing citizens will accept most readily. The more that these three views of policing have in common, the more likely a mutually supportive interaction will result.

Performance criteria in any organization must mirror the organization's mission and the type of training or orientation received by employees. Whether the organization has a service-delivery function or a sales quota, performance must be judged by its stated purpose. Without such agreement the employees could not be held responsible for meeting the employer's mission. In police organizations the primary mission is well-accepted, and that is to protect life. How lives are protected and what is done outside life-threatening situations, however, is not so clear. Police organizations recruit, select and hire individuals who hold a variety of ideas about police work, and how it should be conducted. Some officers maintain a "Joe Friday" approach to police work which requires that everything be done by the book. Others are more like "Dirty Harry" who believes that the end product of bringing someone to justice justifies the means of police work. On the one hand, an officer may believe that, if by following proper procedures and policies he or she loses a case, it is still good police work. On the other hand, another officer may look at a lost case as unacceptable. This second officer thinks we should do anything to punish a "bad guy" regardless of the rules, and disagrees when a suspect is released for some procedural problem. This dilemma must be solved at the Chief's level with orders concerning the rights of defendants and enforcement of appropriate sanctions for those who do not follow them.

The above examples leave little room for disagreement. A more problematic issue has to do with *how* to police. It is much easier to assess police performance by straightforward empirical measures such as traffic tickets or criminal arrests, than the subjective evaluations of a supervisor concerning a police officer's style or demeanor. If a police officer were judged strictly on a numerical count of tickets or arrests, and that officer wanted to improve his or her evaluation, it is obvious what must be done. Logically, there would be numerous tickets and arrests which would not hold up in court, creating all sorts of delays and generating all sorts of complaints. Perhaps it would be better to reward officers for only *good* tickets and arrests, and take points away for tickets and arrests that are challenged successfully. This approach also has its problems. Under this scheme, an officer might lose points for making an arrest that was questionable under legal standards, but that was for the safety of the community. Similarly, a traffic ticket which was issued for the safety of the driver or passenger and was overturned by a court would count negatively for the officer. The impact of such a scheme might deter some officers from issuing questionable tickets or making questionable arrests, but it also might encourage them to issue excessive tickets or make many arrests to counteract the questionable ones. One way to consider both measures would be to take the ratio of prosecutions to arrest, but that would introduce a whole new set of conditions over which the officer has no control. The success of the process is also dependent upon the desires of officers to be evaluated by empirical measures.

The logical alternative, the qualitative measures, lend themselves to manipulation and interpretation which can be based on loyalty, friendship, or some criterion other than good policing. And even if some safeguards were possible, a police officer's actions may be acceptable in one situation but not another. These subtle differences may be obvious, but they are difficult to grade, record and evaluate. For example, an officer questioning an individual about a serious crime may interpret his antagonistic behavior as guilt or at least suspicious and become insistent, rude, or even nasty toward this individual. The suspect may interpret the officer's behavior as out-of-line and inform the officer of this discourteous behavior, however, in much stronger words. This hypothetical scenario is moving toward an unhealthy conclusion. In real life, the suspect is likely to back down and allow the officer to "win" the confrontation. He may, however, push the officer into a challenge and a potentially violent encounter. If the suspect were the "bad guy," or if he were some honest citizen in a bad mood, should the officer intimidate or act rudely toward him? Is this good policing, or does it fall into the typical macho image some police have created for themselves? As a supervisor, would you rate the officer positively if he acted as outlined above and arrested a felon? Would you rate him the same way if the suspect were a businessman who resembled a suspect, but was in a bad mood because a pending business deal just fell through? These are some of the problems associated with using the qualitative performance measures of policing.

In general, using quantitative performance measures alone

has problems similar to those experienced if only the qualitative measures were used. When looking at police performance or criteria within and between neighborhoods, these problems are magnified, as members of these various communities do not agree on which criteria are most appropriate. We found that police officers within the same department do not even agree on the priority of the criteria to be used. In fact, both civilians and police officers want differential policing depending upon the neighborhood. In areas that acknowledge this need or may desire policing which relates to their neighborhood, it is important that the police department responds and determines the most appropriate style and the limits of policing in each neighborhood. In addition, police officials must determine from within their own ranks what criteria should be used to evaluate the officers. Once this research is conducted and updated periodically, police managers will have an enlightened view of their officers in the community they serve.

Two final components are necessary to complete this phase of enhanced community-based policing. First, the police officers should be educated and trained in the expectations of the communities they serve. They must be aware of differences that may exist between gender or ethnic groups or between social classes in order to bring their own style of policing into line with the expectations of the community and the department. Second, community members should be encouraged to provide feedback to the police department on its individual officers and on general department performance. This feedback loop will assure that top-level policymakers know what is expected or demanded in different communities. Specific suggestions for this information transfer will be made later.

Depending upon the size and type of the police department and the areas to be served, police administrators may want to explore the possibility of establishing or maintaining satellite units which have some autonomy from central headquarters. The degree of autonomy necessarily will depend on many variables. In our study, it became evident that some autonomy would be possible in several of the neighborhoods we studied, but difficult to administer in others. To make matters even more problematic, if existing reporting areas or sectors crossed several neighborhood boundaries, it might be useful to educate and train officers in some of the neighborhood's expectations rather than attempt to decentralize or reorganize a well-established district. Since our study was limited to five specific neighborhoods, it would be necessary to gain further knowledge about surrounding areas before anything more than general conclusions can be made.

The fundamental decision on how much control there should be for central management and how much control should be allocated to line supervisors certainly deserves further attention. One of the most important considerations is that the missions of the police are not lost in organizational shuffles.

8

Conclusions: Attitudes toward the Police and Policing

Many of the conclusions discussed so far concerning police task evaluations apply well to this section. Neighborhood differences in attitudes toward the policing are as large as the differences in task evaluations. It is very clear that there is more variation in attitudes toward police practices among neighborhoods than within the neighborhoods. In fact, we found a surprising degree of consensus within neighborhoods. In all of our scales, with the exception of the demeanor scale, there is enough variation among neighborhoods to suggest some differences in police practices, in at least one of the neighborhoods. Further, a comparison of these different neighborhood profiles with the attitudes of the police indicate that the police have views quite congruent with some neighborhoods and quite incongruent with others. *Probably our most important conclusion is that residence in a specific neighborhood is a more influential factor than gender or ethnicity in explaining variation in attitudes toward policing.* On each of our five attitude scales concerning the police and the scales concerning different professionals in the criminal justice system, there are significant neighborhood differences. However, gender and ethnic differences are minimal in all of these relationships. Apparently, neighborhood climate and the frequent interactions of people in close association are much more influential in forming attitudes toward the police than gender or ethnicity. This finding alone has important implications. Apparently, in a highly stratified, multi-ethnic metropolitan center like Miami, neighborhood climate not only varies tremendously, but strongly influences one's perceptions of the police and styles of policing. It is true that the police can function fairly well at times by responding to these differences by relying upon the understanding and ability of the individual officer. However, this places a tremendous burden and responsibility on the individual officer who may lack either the knowledge of the various neighborhood culture or not have the ability to figure out the most appropriate and effective response. The individual officer may lack the incentive to go through this rather difficult process on his or her own. It is obvious that assistance from the police administration would be very helpful if not crucial in setting this process in motion. The police officer's effectiveness could be enhanced greatly if he received training specific to his district. The training would include knowledge concerning unique characteristics of the neighborhoods in the officer's district and the most appropriate and effective policing styles for those neighborhoods.

In this context, it is important to note that attitudes about different styles of policing do not vary among the officers assigned to the different districts in the department. Apparently, officers do not modify their styles of policing significantly when working in different districts. It is interesting to find assignment by district to be irrelevant in explaining the attitudes of the police. This indicates that police in the different neighborhoods apparently do not have different styles of policing to match the unique characteristics of the neighborhoods. Similar behavior displayed by police officers in one area may be met with approval, while it may be met with disapproval in another neighborhood. Officers should be trained to understand that their demeanor can be viewed as appropriate or not appropriate depending upon the neighborhood in which they are working.

One good example of unique neighborhood characteristics that could translate into policing style involves the Cuban neighborhoods. The Cuban neighborhoods perceived police demeanor much more positively than the other neighborhoods. By educating the police working in these neighborhoods to realize the considerable citizen support they enjoy, we could reduce the normal level of mistrust and incorrect interpretations surrounding police-citizen encounters. In many situations, police officers believe that they are perceived as acting inappropriately when this is not the case. What may result is a vicious cycle of inaccurate perceptions between police and the public that may lead to unnecessary confrontations. In fact, the two groups of Cubans report the most positive demeanor, even more so than the Anglo sample from Kendall or the police themselves. The groups having the least positive perception of police demeanor include the students, residents of Rolling Oaks, the Mariels and residents of James Scott housing project.

Another unique characteristic of the Cuban neighborhoods is that these residents were the only ones who agree that the responsibility for crime control rests mainly with the police. This characteristic suggests two policing strategies. The style of policing in these neighborhoods should reflect the citizens' strong reliance on the police for crime control. Further, police should educate these residents to understand how citizens can assist the police in increasing the effectiveness of their crime control efforts. Knowledge of these attitudes can help officers in Cuban neighborhoods interact with citizens more effectively, and at the same time help direct new initiatives in that area through crime watch or other community programs.

Residents of the Cuban neighborhoods were the only respondents, with the exception of the police, who feel that it is appropriate for police on patrol to stop and question suspicious-looking citizens. These respondents also agreed that these active patrol strategies might be more appropriate in some neighborhoods to control crime than in others. Police officers can expect more support of, and less resistance to, active patrol strategies in the Cuban neighborhoods. In the other neighborhoods where residents disapprove of these patrol strategies, officers will need to use more discretion and possibly incorporate positive community encounters with citizens to minimize negative reactions to active patrolling.

Using the Cuban neighborhoods as an example, then, it becomes clear how finding unique neighborhood characteristics can aid the patrol officer in increasing his/her effectiveness in different neighborhoods. It is a process of gaining a better understanding of unique neighborhood characteristics and then training officers to be aware of them and how to select the most effective strategies for police-citizen encounters.

Another finding that has important implications for police-community relations and effective policing is that there exists a general agreement among all groups, that to be effective, police must use discretion in following police procedures. This finding indicates considerable citizen support for individualized community policing styles. Citizens realize that the police sometimes need to use their discretion differently in different neighborhoods, and they apparently approve. It is interesting to note that the police did not agree as strongly with this idea as the residents in most of the neighborhoods. The two Cuban neighborhoods were more in agreement with this idea while the residents of Rolling Oaks and the police had the weakest level of agreement. Apparently, the police do not recognize the level of general support for their authority and the use of discretion that exists in the community, especially the level found in the Cuban neighborhoods.

However, the use of discretion is not accepted without reservation. All of the groups, with the exception of James Scott residents, *dis*agreed with the use of discretion when it is based on ethnicity. Most respondents felt that it is inappropriate to view one ethnic group or the other as more crime prone or suspicious. Apparently, it is felt that neighborhood distinctions are sometimes necessary, even when the neighborhood has a fairly distinct ethnic composition. However, the distinction should be based on factors other than ethnicity, such as crime rate, attitudes toward the police, etc. It seems to follow, then, that no ethnic group should be viewed as suspicious in the low crime areas.

Citizens' attitudes toward police and policing can be instrumental in shaping police practices, training, and the eventual impact of the police upon different neighborhoods. However, these perceptions should not be evaluated in a vacuum. The next section places these perceptions into a larger social context.

TRI-LEVEL ANALYSIS

Our data indicate a pattern of general support for the police in most neighborhoods, compared to other aspects of the criminal justice and social systems. Attitudes are more positive as we move from the social system and criminal justice system level to the more specific level of police. It is interesting that the attitudes of most citizens toward the police are not as negative as many believe them to be. In fact, the police fare much better in the public's eye than the criminal justice system as a whole, and better than the overall social system.

It is the neighborhood comprised of Cubans who came to Miami during the 1960s that reports the most positive attitudes toward all three levels of society (the social system, criminal justice system and police), especially toward the police.

Our findings indicate that those who show considerable support for the police are not people who simply have positive attitudes towards all institutions in our society. Most have some special regard for the police. In many cases, strong supporters of the police will be quite negative about other aspects of the social or criminal justice systems.

The converse analysis also speaks well for the police. Most individuals with negative attitudes toward the police also hold negative attitudes toward the entire criminal justice system. Apparently, negative attitudes about the police, unlike positive attitudes, emanate from and are closely tied to one's attitudes toward the entire system of criminal justice. These negative attitudes are part of a set of attitudes that cluster around the broader legal system and perhaps even include the political system. Programs that are designed to change responses to the police which ignore this larger attitude complex are unlikely to yield impressive results.

The police may feel the impact of these negative attitudes more directly than others in the criminal justice system because of the more frequent and direct interaction between police and citizens. The policeman is frequently in an adversary relationship with his public. It is reasonable to suggest that individuals or groups who feel alienated from the political process or who believe the justice system is unresponsive to their needs, might transfer their dissatisfaction to the agents of that system most visible to them—the police.

A general implication of our findings is that it is apparent from our analyses of attitudes toward three levels of the social structure that attitudes directed toward each level can be very divergent. Further, it is clear that attitudes toward the different levels are interrelated in several ways. First, attitudes toward one level (i.e., police) may be nested in attitudes toward a more general level (i.e., the justice system). Second, attitudes toward a more general level (i.e., social institutions in general) may indicate a generally positive or generally negative orientation that provides the basis for interpreting the attitudes toward a more specific level (i.e., the police).

If researchers fail to give due attention to significant features of the larger attitude complex, interpretations of the attitudes will be out of context and possibly biased. This work is just a beginning in sorting out the more general attitude complex and its relationship to attitudes toward the police. Further research should develop standard measures and procedures to accomplish this goal.

In the samples we studied, the data confirm for the police Lipset and Schneider's (1983) finding that people have more positive attitudes concerning local representatives of an institution when compared to the levels that are more removed. The police, being the most frequently confronted professionals in the criminal justice system, enjoy the highest levels of approval.

Lipset and Schneider (1983:125) also concluded that each institution has its own social and political bases of support. Patterns of support for institutions across the population tend to be specific and distinct for each institution. They report that shifts in confidence over time tend to be broad, general and responsive to events in the external environment, but that there is no specific location of overall "confidence" per se. Our findings from Miami are contrary to their conclusion. Cubans as a group report much stronger levels of support *at all three levels*: the police, the criminal justice system, and social institutions in general. Even though the Cubans as a group are extremely supportive of the police and serve as their basis of support in Miami, it is important to interpret this support in the context of their generally positive orientation toward all three levels. When focusing on negative attitudes toward the police, we found that they are firmly nested in negative attitudes about the criminal justice system as a whole. However, they do not correspond closely to negative attitudes concerning social institutions in general. This conclusion points to the necessity of putting negative attitudes toward the police in the context of attitudes toward the criminal justice system. It also adds another dimension when interpreting attitudes toward the police: one's orientation toward social institutions in general.

These conclusions, as well as those presented earlier, can be translated into information for police managers and for police officer training. The more that is known about a specific neighborhood, the better prepared police can be to control crime, maintain order, and provide services which are all approved and appreciated by residents.

A FINAL COMMENT

Conclusions specific to each of our findings have been discussed above. From these conclusions, we have drawn some overall insights into policing in different neighborhoods. We have noticed that two minority groups have different orientations toward the police. The blacks and the Cubans share their status as minority groups, but report completely different conceptual views of their relationship to the police. Even though there are important differences between blacks in the middle-class neighborhood and the poor blacks, overall they are much more negative and suspicious toward the police than the Cubans. Apparently, they do not view the police as their agents of social control, and perceive a disjuncture between the formal control system and their system of informal control. Rather, they tend to view the police as representatives of the majority class. This is an especially interesting finding in light of the numerous differences between the two black neighborhoods. In spite of their different views on specific issues, they share this general conflict orientation.

In contrast, residents of the two Cuban neighborhoods tended to be very positive and trusting of the police. Even the 1980 entrants from the Port of Mariel, most of whom are lower-class and severely disadvantaged, report generally positive attitudes toward the police and policing. This raises a significant question: why does this lower-class group conceptualize police as their agents, when the blacks do not? Perhaps the blacks view themselves as being victimized by society, while the Cubans, as new immigrants, view themselves as fortunate to be in a society where the police have any concern for the rights of the underclass.

Within the black community, our two neighborhoods differed in one important respect: residents of the middle-class neighborhood reported attitudes toward the police with small variations, while residents of the poor black neighborhood reported polarized attitudes toward the police. One group reported positive attitudes toward the general social system, yet negative attitudes toward the police. The other group reported negative attitudes toward the major social institutions and positive attitudes toward the police. It appears that within this lower-class black neighborhood, there is a group of law-abiding citizens who are constantly victimized by their neighbors. These citizens are positive toward the police, and in fact, rely heavily upon the police for their protection against what they fear the most, black-on-black crime. This group shares with other blacks the general negativity toward most institutions, but because of their reliance upon the police, they have formed a bond of trust. The other group, the stereotypical poor black, is more suspicious of the police and views them as working against their interests.

Overall, our findings support the validity of the neighborhood concept as a social unit with respect to attitudes toward the police and policing. In addition, we found support for the need to base policing strategies and practices upon neighborhood characteristics. Of course, this does not hold for all neighborhoods, but it is important for homogeneous neighborhoods which have attitudes and values divergent from the police. Finally, the interactive model helps to clarify the relationship between residents of these diverse neighborhood cultures and the police. Analysis of the interaction between the informal system of social control at the neighborhood level and the formal system of the police is a productive approach to better understand police-community relationships and to structure policing strategies and policies at the local level.

9

Policing in the Community

This final chapter will integrate our major findings and conclusions into policy-related proposals. While these suggestions are derived from our present study, they are also grounded in findings and conclusions from other research and consequently have important implications for police departments and municipalities in cities and states across the country.

The duties and expectations of the police are extremely complex as our previous discussion has demonstrated. There is neither a clear-cut set of rules for the police to follow nor is there a predetermined set of expectations that citizens can use to evaluate the police. Not only are police charged with the duty of protecting lives, but they are charged with maintaining order, enforcing the law, and providing a variety of social services. It is the way in which officers perform their duties and achieve their goals that we have referred to as style.

In a society as diverse as ours, there are bound to be diffeent priorities placed on these demands by different people who live in different geographic areas and perhaps within these same jurisdictions. In addition, police officers are not all the same, do not have similar opinions or expectations, do not have the same style and do not perform at the same level. In fact, police departments may operate under a number of separate philosophies. These differences all influence the policies which allocate resources and ultimately determine how a police department and its officers operate in the neighborhoods they serve.

Given the different character of our cities and our neighborhoods, police administrators must decide how to allocate their scarce resources. In other words, administrators have to make policies concerning how well-trained the officers are going to be, in what they will be trained, how they will be deployed, what their enforcement priorities will be, and what tactics they will use. This requires administrators to place priorities on police officers' use of time, choice of activities, and overall style of dealing with the public.

A strategic factor in the administration of resources is the style of law enforcement desired by the community that is served by the police department. Citizen leaders can set reasonable boundaries on police actions, and these usually depend upon the social, economic and political characteristics of the community. Police chiefs must respond to the differences among communities and should balance the tasks their officers perform to include the conceptual categories of order-maintenance, law enforcement and service which Wilson (1968) painstakingly analyzed.

Related to categories and styles of policing is the use of police discretion. This is certainly an important topic for police scholars and administrators to understand and control, because it shapes the type of policing which is found within a community by permitting administrators and officers to use formal and informal methods of social control (Davis, 1975). More important than a discussion of conceptual categories of police, or police discretion, is an analysis of the social distance between police and the community, which has implications for the effectiveness of law enforcement and police organization. Creating policing strategies which are based upon these neighborhood differences must include both administrative and street-level decisions. At both levels, the most effective strategies need to be identified and organized. Once these strategies are selected as the most appropriate to serve the police mission, they are managed and implemented at the street level as specific tasks and ways to perform the tasks.

Earlier this strategy was referred to as integrating the formal and informal systems of social control which exist within neighborhoods. The *informal social control* in the residential context refers to the development, observance, and enforcement of local norms for appropriate public behavior. It is the process by which individual behavior is influenced by a group, and usually functions to maintain a level of predictability and control in the behavior of group members, and to promote the well-being of the group as a whole.

Formal social control is based on written rules or laws and prescribed punishments for violating these rules and laws. The police and the courts are the institutions most directly charged with maintaining order under formal social controls. The means of formal social control are not very effective without the direct support of the informal means of control. The positive consequences and desired results of a combination and interaction of the two is a central finding of this research. It is this integration which can guide the creation, adoption and acceptance of the styles of policing which will be most effective.

Another way of exploring this relationship between a social institution and its social environment is to examine its productivity. Jeffrey Slovak (1986: 8-11) explains how productivity, innovation, and growth are contingent on the fit between an institution's internal structure and its environment. Slovak argues that more generally, stuctural and functional facets of an organization are critically subject to external control and that pure organizational survival is contingent on the character of the environmental niche that the organization occupies. This relationship between organization and its environment is especially critical for the police. Albert Reiss and David Bordua (1967) have argued:

All organizations can be so studied, of course, but . . . the police have as their fundamental task the creation and maintenance of, and their participation in, external relationships. Indeed, the central meaning of police authority itself is its significance as a mechanism for "managing" relationships (pp. 25-26).

By far, the greatest component of the environment of a police agency is the consumers of police services or the citizens the agency serves. Unfortunately, this important component of the environment is highly segmented and varied. Effective policing requires the police organization to be critically aware of, and in tune with, the nuances of its environment. Police officers are able to carry out their mandates in a variety of different ways. On the one hand, officers can be coarse, macho and demeaning to citizens whom they arrest or serve. On the other hand, officers can treat their "clients" or the consumers of police work with some dignity, respect and sensitivity. This dilemma exists for both crime-fighting duties and service functions performed by the police. We will first discuss crime fighting and then turn to the calls for service.

Jonathan Casper studied criminal defendant's views of police, and reports that the general consensus is

. . . the policeman is himself simply doing a job and is the subject of motives and desires that are not markedly different from those of the defendant. The policeman is basically a worker, not an impartial arbitrator or enforcer. The process of arrest and the activities of police in general are not so much different from street life itself. You get by; you do what you have to to survive; you take shortcuts; you play games with each other. Nobody is neutral or detached or impartial; everyone has his job and he does it. Dealing with people as individuals rather than as objects or adversaries is not part of the system, for the production ethic and the organizational structure militate against it (1972: 49–50).

It is the strongly reinforced need to produce, and the traditional organizational reward systems that discourage the police officer from treating consumers as individuals. Police officers must take control of every situation which has the potential for a confrontation or violence. How they take control, or the style they use usually sets the tone of the interaction. We know from prior research (Sykes and Brent, 1980), that there exists a continuum of control which moves from definitional to imperative to coercive. In other words, an officer will attempt to take control of any confrontation and this is usually accomplished by defining the situation. If this strategy does not work the officer may order or command the citizen, or use force as a last resort.

Not all officers react appropriately by attempting to control citizens verbally. Often, the verbal control escalates too quickly and a situation that could have been resolved with ease erupts into a violent one. It is paramount that an officer understand that his best weapon is his skill to negotiate, it is his mouth, not his weapon (Alpert, 1985). To complicate matters, the same words spoken by different officers to different defendants may mean different things. Data available in the intercultural communications literature demonstrate the need to look beyond the simple police-citizen confrontation. Questions include who is the officer, how does he or she present himself, what kind of mood is he or she in, is he or she Anglo, black or Hispanic? And the citizen, is he or she intimidated, upset, under the influence of some substance, etc.

It is the interaction of these statuses or effects that must be analyzed if we want to arrive at a clearer picture. Several researchers have attempted to observe police-citizen confrontations and comment upon the outcomes, but due to the complicated nature of the data collection and analysis, no concrete findings have been published (see McIver and Parks, 1983; and Brown, 1981: 142-145). Although limited to a select number of variables, the data from the present study demonstrate that neighborhood identity explains significant differences in citizens' attitudes about policing and the rankings of tasks for evaluating the police. The ethnicity of police officers explains the police officers' own attitudes and rankings of evaluation criteria.

STYLES OF POLICING

Police officers are involved in order-maintenance and service-delivery as well as law enforcement. Providing these services to the public involves more of an officer's time than does the crime fighting, and also involves a different relationship between officer and citizen. It has been argued that police service should be delivered in a style quite different from that used to fight crimes, but even crime-fighting activities can be carried out in a civilized and professional manner. Citizens who contact the police are most often in need of help, assistance or direction. Although our data indicate that both police officers and citizens hold courtesy, demeanor and judgment as very important elements of success, there is no monitoring or institutionalized system to acknowledge or reward this style of policing. There are differences in attitudes both within and between the police and groups of citizens.

Police style can be strongly influenced by departmental or individual characteristics, although precious little attention has been focused on the individual-level analysis (McIver and Parks, 1983; Muir, 1977). Wilson (1968) argues that decisions of patrolmen are shaped significantly by the administrative style of the chief of police. In turn, a single operational style will be associated with different police departments. Perhaps the chief's influence is an important consideration (see Geller, 1985), but our data and that of other studies indicate that there is a great deal more to a policeman's style. Michael Brown studied officers in several police departments and commented that:

Regardless of the expectations of administrators, every patrolman must still come to terms with the pressures of the police bureaucracy—the disjuncture between rewards and performance, the punitive style of supervision and control, and the pressure to reconcile the substantive and instrumental goals of police work (1981: 239).

Brown's research suggests that uncertain and ambiguous administrative control which is characteristic of small police departments leads to a pattern of leniency or lack of control over the officers. He concludes that small police departments, in order to gain public support, may have to lose some autonomy from community politics and community pressure. Smaller police departments compared to the larger ones (and cities) are more likely to have their law enforcement priorities and style of policing influenced by members of the local communities. This is not to say that all police officer behavior will be strongly influenced, but only that a general philosophy is more likely to be affected. In the larger departments, however, it is more likely that the Chief will set the priorities and general style. Even in these larger departments, the relationship between the Chief and his boss (whether it be the city manager, mayor, county manager, etc.) is problematic. For example, an elected sheriff should be more responsible to the public than to a board of county commissioners, while an appointed chief may have his loyalties in another direction (Brown, 1981; Skolnick and Bayley, 1986).

This discussion has moved us away from our primary purpose, but has taken us to an important, although preliminary conclusion. Our study found that within a large metropolitan police department, significant differences exist among the officers and between the officers and members of the community. The major explanatory variable among the officers was ethnicity while the most important variable among the officers and citizens was neighborhood. In our homogeneous neighborhoods it was possible to identify law enforcement needs, consumer preferences and political realities. Perhaps it is in this unit, the neighborhood, that the most effective and efficient policing can take place. The community-oriented policing concept which met with mixed success should be reexamined and reorganized to meet today's needs (see Greene and Taylor, 1987; Goldstein, 1987; Sherman, 1986; and Smith, 1986). The data from our study suggest that no less than three different styles of policing are necessary to police effectively in our five neighborhoods. This suggests that differential organization would benefit policing as would training pertaining to specific consumer demands and priorities. While our study focused upon homogeneous groups our findings have implications for mixed neighborhoods as well.

FROM TEAM POLICING TO COMMUNITY-BASED POLICING

Team policing was initiated in the Metro-Dade police department in the early 1980s as a response to poor police-community relations, especially in the black community. Prior to the Arthur McDuffie incident, police officers had become accustomed to tension within black communities. In fact, police response calls to these communities often involved planned tactics which required multiple units to respond and to provide security. Citizens soon came to associate police presence with hostility. The

Metro-Dade police administrators asked for volunteer officers to be assigned to some of the most alienated housing projects. In August 1980, four officers began what was to become Metro's team-policing squad. These officers (two Anglo and two black) worked quickly and developed the beginning of a positive relationship between police and these community members. The officers were careful to explain that while they wanted to improve the image of the police, their main job was to enforce laws and protect the law-abiding citizens. These officers were joined by others and the team-policing approach spread to other locations. These teams were supervised closely but had to learn from a trial-and-error approach. Although the officers were immersing themselves in the culture of the community and were developing important linkages, they were not operating with specific organizational mandates or goals. There certainly was a great need for organizational planning and modeling: it was the beginning of a trend in local policing. The remainder of this chapter will focus upon how the police organization can move from a team policing concept to problem-oriented policing to a community-based approach to policing.

MODELS OF POLICE ORGANIZATION

There have been numerous models of police organization that have been espoused over the years (Tansik and Elliott, 1981). One in particular, which fits our findings and those of other research, involves some degree of decentralization and can revolve around the team concept or identification of specific problems, but moves beyond both. Specifically, policing with neighborhood administrative control appears to be the best of several worlds. This model is grounded partly in the community control movement of the 1960s, but guards against total political decentralization. It moves beyond the established research on police which emphasizes deterrence, and focuses upon the impact of the differences among police officers and their actions within their communities.

Positive Policing

During the past ten to fifteen years, many large, urban police departments have adopted some sort of community-oriented policing in response to the demand for decentralization of their police operations.

In theory, community-oriented policing is an excellent way to increase the efficiency and effectiveness of policing, both proactive and reactive. To modify partially their behavior to the demands of the community they serve, and to help officers emphasize non-adversarial problem solving, community or neighborhood-oriented policing, as we see it, includes not only administrative decentralization which may already exist, but appropriate training and institutionalized monitoring and rewards.

Our suggestion of positive policing has several organizational elements which must be added to the traditional components which exist in many community-oriented policing units, to become truely neighborhood based. Most departments stress the need for police officers to return to the old meaning of "beat officer." That is, to learn about the residents and business people from their neighborhoods and see them and be seen in situations that are not always defined as negative or at best neutral (see Reiss, 1985). Whether or not that is achieved, however, is the magic question. Our model, which stresses good relations with the community, requires several key elements. First, to reduce isolation between police and the citizens, officers must be assigned for an extended period, supervised by command staff and advised by neighborhood groups. This move toward stability will increase the identification of an officer with the residents, geography, politics and other issues of a given neighborhood. Second, there must be the traditional police-neighborhood relations meetings or citizens' advisory groups. At this point, our research suggests that even when these two elements are operating, successful neighborhood policing requires proper training, feedback mechanisms, and an institutionalized reward system.

Neighborhood Training

Neighborhood training involves two basic elements: what to do and how to do it. In other words, the priority of police resources, whether fighting crime or providing social services, changes from neighborhood to neighborhood. Police officers must recognize these needs from the consumers' perspectives from that of the police administration and from their own experiences and expectations. Neighborhood training can effectively inform the officer as to what he or she can expect from the residents, physical surroundings or other influences. This in-service training can introduce officers to these community characteristics while working the streets under supervision (in a way similar to a field training officer). The "what-to-do" can be addressed by top-level administrators from both the central headquarters and the neighborhoods. The "how-to-do-it" is the all-important style of policing which we have discussed above. There exist clear differences among officers and citizens concerning style. We believe that matching the style of policing and the neighborhood needs and requirements will improve both the police and the community. This can be achieved through training based upon knowledge of neighborhood values and beliefs as well as the attitudes and priorities of police officers. Research on both the police themselves and the community are necessary elements of this model.

Monitoring and Rewarding

The final recommendations for our proposed model include the institutionalized monitoring and formal reward system. This requires an ongoing system to monitor both the neighborhood and the police (see Furstenberg and Wellford, 1973). The needs of the community can be determined by periodic social surveys which, if linked to census data and local planning information, can inform officials of the changing nature of a given neighborhood. While it is relatively easy to identify what constitutes negative behavior, it is difficult to specify exemplary behavior. The proper use of good research, including appropriate sampling and a panel design, could provide a clear snapshot of the needs expressed by a given neighborhood. Police officers and administrators can work together to identify issues and questions which can answer them. A Blue Ribbon committee studying the Miami Police Department came to a similar conclusion. In its final report (Overtown Blue Ribbon Committee, 1984: 199), it noted:

It is our conclusion that a minor organizational change can have a major impact on community relations and on the interrelationships between citizens and police. We believe that confidence in the police will be enhanced if the police measure and make more visible the activities they perform. Moreover, police work is usually rewarded by the gratitude an officer receives from those who he or she helps. Status in the department, promotions, raises, commendations, etc., rest largely on his or her crime-fighting activities, the number of arrests, crimes he or she solves, etc. As a result, the patrol officer may regard service calls as a necessary evil.

This type of data together with normal law enforcement information and planning meetings, could create and maintain neighborhood profiles. A comparison of officials' views of the community and the community members' views of themselves will provide another element that will improve policing and the quality of life in a community.

Our model is not complete without an informational feedback loop. Both the crime fighting and the service function of the police need to be evaluated on the institutional and individual levels. First, an ongoing study of victimization will provide police with data on how well their system is providing services. Usually, this information is gleaned from official crime statistics (UCR), but this process is doomed to failure (O'Brien, 1985). A survey of crime victims can provide the whole criminal justice system with a needed evaluation. Second, a random survey of consumers of police services can provide administrators and planners with feedback on their services and the officers who provide it. This feedback can serve a dual function at the institutional and individual level.

Rewarding the Police Officer

Most police departments provide incentives for their officers. These include traditional promotions, merit increases, and "officer-of-the-month" recognition. Many departments offer several opportunities for their officers to receive or earn rewards. Traditionally, these rewards have been based upon aggressive actions which have led to an arrest(s), the capture of a dangerous felon, or some other heroic activity. These criteria for rewarding police officers are important and serve to encourage similar actions from others. Yet, there are other types of police behavior which deserve recognition, but remain lost and hidden behind the visible, aggressive activities of police officers. These activities which should receive more attention include exemplary service to the community and the reduction and diffusion of violence. Those who provide meritorious service have been recognized but often their actions are lost behind the brave shooting incident or heroic rescue. There needs to be local recognition for officers who serve their "beat" or neighborhood in an exemplary fashion. A "Best Cop on the Block" recognition would be an important reward, if provided by local residents or merchants. The officer who *avoids* a shooting or *talks* a suspect into custody may not have his actions known to his superiors, and when they are, the officer may be labelled as a "chicken" or one who cannot provide needed backup to his fellow officers. It is this behavior, constant with neighborhood norms, which must receive attention and reinforcement. It is the nonaggressive, violent-avoiding behavior which needs to be reinforced, rewarded and established as the model for other officers to copy.

An institutional reward system should be established for officers who avoid or reduce violent situations, and who avoid the use of force, especially deadly force when it is justifiable. Once command officers, from the Chief to the sergeants, support and reward violence reduction, it is possible to enlist the support of private business and service groups to provide symbolic and monetary rewards for such behavior. The institutional support for the effective policing of a neighborhood can only encourage others to consider a change in priorities and a style. While this is only one aspect of our Positive Policing model, it could serve as a successful step toward meeting the joint needs of both the citizens and the police.

Toward an Interactive Model

Police departments around the country have instituted one or more of these organizational components into community-

Figure 9-1.
Model for Effective Neighborhood-based Policing

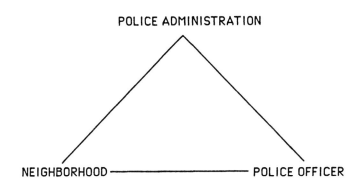

POLICE ADMINISTRATION

NEIGHBORHOOD ———————————— POLICE OFFICER

oriented policing programs, but we were unable to locate any program which incorporated them all; and it is the cumulative effect of *all* the information which can really improve policing. In fact, having a team, problem or community-oriented policing project without proper planning, training and administration may be more harmful than not having one at all (Skolnick and Bayley, 1986; Mastrofski, 1983). The mere existence of a special unit to provide special services may raise the expectations of the community members. When these expectations are not met, then there can be a backlash effect of disapproval and disappointment. There is a requirement that all component parts of the model are coordinated and feed into each other and are analyzed individually and as a total effect.

As demonstrated in Figure 9-1, effective neighborhood policing requires that police administrators acquire adequate information of the specific neighborhood. This includes a knowledge of the informal control structure of the neighborhood, attitudes about the police, policing strategies and styles. This information can be obtained from citizen surveys, census data, community advisory groups and from neighborhood leaders. After accumulating the information, police administrators can decide how to deal with any incongruence between the neighborhood context and police policies, strategies and styles. Some of these differences can be reduced by campaigns to educate the citizens and change public opinion and attitudes. In other cases, discrepancies can be reduced by training programs for officers who are assigned to the areas. The training can focus on neighborhood-specific strategies, appropriate styles for the specific neighborhood and placing priorities on tasks consistent with the neighborhood's expectations. Subsequent to appropriate neighborhood-based training, police administrators need to create and institutionalize a system of monitoring and rewarding police officers' behavior. The police officers assigned to the neighborhood provide the final link integrating the formal control system of the police with the informal system in the neighborhood. Officers must apply the training principles appropriately through their use of discretion.

From data collected from the neighborhoods, a good plan for Positive Policing can bring modern police work in line with our modern world. Moore and Kelling have summarized our ideas quite well:

Police strategies do not exist in a vacuum. They are shaped by important legal, political, and attitudinal factors, as well as by local resources and capabilities, all factors which now sustain the modern conception of policing. So there may be little leeway for modern police executives. But the modern conception of policing is in serious trouble, and a review of the nature of that trouble against the background of the American history of policing gives a clear direction to police forces that wish to improve their performance as crime fighters and public servants.

The two fundamental features of a new police strategy must be these: that the role of private citizens in the control of crime and maintenance of public order be established and encouraged, not derided and thwarted, and that the police become more active, accessible participants in community affairs. The police will have to do little to encourage citizens to participate in community policing, for Americans are well practiced at undertaking private, voluntary efforts; all they need to know is that the police force welcomes and supports such activity. Being more visible and accessible is slightly more difficult, but hiring more "community relations" specialists is surely not the answer. Instead, the police must get out of their cars, and spend more time in public spaces such as parks and plazas, confronting and assisting citizens with their private troubles. This is mundane, prosaic work but it probably beats driving around in cars waiting for a radio call. Citizens would surely feel safer and, perhaps, might even be safer (1983: 65).

Our model will work most effectively in homogeneous neighborhoods, and in areas where police administrators have strong control of their officers. It is important that police officers work for the community, not merely to impress their supervisors. That is why it is so important for community members to provide information to police administrators. Homogeneity, in our research, crosses ethnic boundaries and in some cases social class distinctions. Therefore, it is an attitudinal or ideological homogeneity which is an essential element of our model. Some cities will find it quite reasonable to split police jurisdictions to use the proposed model, as many geographic locations attract or limit certain groups of people. Other cities may find their demographic mixture just too complex to divide a police jurisdiction for this type of policing. Regardless of the administrative level of commitment, patrol officers can be in the best position to understand the varied and changing needs of the community, and with input from research and training, appropriate activities can be devised to control crime and provide service. Our model utilizes the individual officer's talents and experiences to provide expert assistance to the neighborhood. It is they who can provide a sense of balance to community relations within the context of law enforcement. The structure of the police administration determines how much influence the police officer has in his or her patrol area. It is our suggestion that a police department incorporate a total commitment to neighborhood intervention and community evaluation. There is a price to pay for such enhanced community involvement in policing. This price tag includes chipping away at some traditional police activities and perhaps adding or changing administrative controls. In addition, research shows that citizens who have confidence and trust in the police will take a more active role in reporting crime than those citizens who do not have confidence or trust in the police. This is likely to lead to a higher reported crime rate and the corresponding need for more officers and a greater capacity to process criminals through the justice system (Dukes and Alpert, 1980). There is an additional economic price to pay for data collection, data analysis and the special police training that we have discussed. It is our belief, to coin an old phrase, that a jurisdiction will pay now or pay later. Policing in America must move beyond its current level. We have the knowledge, we have the means, so all we need now is the commitment.

Unfortunately, there is no guarantee that this model or any other reform will be an acceptable answer to a yet unsolved problem. It is, however, a move to something Sir Robert Peel would have been proud to see.

References

Albrecht, Stan, and Miles Green. Attitudes Toward the Police and the Larger Attitude Complex. *Criminology* 15 (1977): 67–86.

Alderson, J. C. The Police in the 1980s: Influences of New Social Perspectives on the Organization and Role of the Police. *Political Science Abstracts* 10, no. 1 (1982): i-vi.

Allen, David, and Michael Maxfield. Judging Police Performance: Views and Behavior of Patrol Officers. In R. Bennett (ed.) *Police At Work: Issues and Analysis.* Beverly Hills: Sage Publications, 1983. Pp. 65–86.

Alpert, Geoffrey P. *The American System of Criminal Justice.* Beverly Hills: Sage Publications. 1985.

———. Police Use of Deadly Force: The Miami Experience. In R. Dunham and G. Alpert (eds.) *Policing America: Readings in Contemporary Law Enforcement.* Prospect Heights, Ill.: Waveland Press. 1989. Chapter 28.

Alpert, Geoffrey P., and Roger Dunham. Keeping Academically Marginal Youths in School: A Prediction Model. *Youth and Society* 17, no. 4 (June 1986): 346–361.

———. *Policing Urban America.* Prospect Heights, Ill.: Waveland Press, 1988.

Alpert, Geoffrey, and D. Hicks. Prisoner's Attitudes Toward Components of the Legal and Judicial Systems. *Criminology* 14 (1977) 461–482.

Apple, Nancy, and David O'Brien. Neighborhood Racial Composition and Residents' Evaluation of Police Performance. *Journal of Police Science and Administration* 11, no. 1 (March 1983): 76–83.

Balch, Robert. The Police Personality: Fact or Fiction? *Journal of Criminal Law, Criminology and Police Science* 63 (1972): 106–119.

Banerjee, Tribid, and William Baer. *Beyond the Neighborhood Unit: Residential Environments and Public Policy.* New York: Plenum Press. 1984.

Banton, Michael. *The Police in the Community.* New York: Basic Books. 1964.

Bayley, David. *Community Policing: A Report From the Devils' Advocate.* Paper presented at the Temple University Criminal Justice Symposium. Philadelphia. May, 1987.

Bennett, Richard. *Police at Work: Issues and Analysis.* Beverly Hills: Sage, 1983.

Benson, Paul. Political Alienation and Public Satisfaction with Police Services. *Pacific Sociological Review* 24 (1981): 45–64.

Bittner, Egon. The Police on Skid Row: A Study of Peacekeeping. *American Sociological Review* 32 (1967): 699–715.

Black, Donald. *The Manners and Customs of the Police.* New York: Academic Press. 1980.

Bloch, Peter, and Donald Anderson. *Policewomen on Patrol.* Washington, D.C.: Police Foundation. 1974.

Bloch, Peter, and David Specht. *Neighborhood Policing.* Washington, D.C.: U.S. Government Printing Office. 1973.

Bordua, David. Juvenile Delinquency and Anomie: An Attempt at Replication. *Social Problems* 6 (1958): 230–238.

Bowers, William, and Jon Hirsch. The Impact of Foot Patrol Staffing on Crime and Disorder in Boston. Paper presented at the First Annual Temple University Criminal Justice Symposium. Philadelphia, 1987.

Boydstun, John E., and Michael Sherry. *San Diego Community Profile: Final Report.* Washington, D.C.: Police Foundation. 1975.

Brodsky, Stanley L., and H. O'Neal Smitherman. *Handbook of Scales for Research in Crime and Delinquency.* New York: Plenum Press. 1983.

Brown, Lee, and Edgar Martin. *Neighborhood Team Policing.* Police Chief, May 1976.

Brown, Lee, and Mary Ann Wykoff, Policing Houston: Reducing Fear and Improving Service. *Crime and Delinquency.* 33 (1987): 71–89.

Brown, Michael. *Working the Street: Police Discretion and the Dilemmas of Reform.* New York: Russell Sage. 1981.

Brown, William. Local Policing: A Three Dimensional Task Analysis. *Journal of Criminal Justice* 3 (1974): 1–16.

Buchanan, James E. *Miami: A Chronological and Documenting History 1517–1972.* New York: Oceana. 1977.

Burbeck, Elizabeth, and Adrian Furnhan. Police Officer Selection. *Journal of Police Sciences and Administration* 13 (1985): 58–69.

Burgess, Ernest. Can Neighborhood Work Have a Scientific Basis? In Robert E. Park and E. Burgess (eds.) *The City*. Chicago: The University of Chicago Press. 1925. Pp. 142–155.

Bursik, Robert, and Jim Webb. Community Change and Patterns of Delinquency. *American Journal of Sociology* 88 (1982): 24–42.

Caplow, Theodore, and Robert Foreman. Neighborhood Interaction in a Homogeneous Community. *American Sociological Review* 15 (1950): 357–366.

Casper, Jonathan. *American Criminal Justice: The Defendant's Perspective*. Englewood Cliffs, N.J.: Prentice-Hall. 1972.

Charles, Michael. The Utilization of Attitude Surveys in the Police Decision Process. *Journal of Police Science and Administration* 8, no. 3 (September 1980): 294–303.

Chilton, Roland. Continuity in Delinquency Area Research: A Comparison of Studies for Baltimore, Detroit and Indianapolis. *American Sociological Review* 29 (1964): 71–83.

City of Miami. *Overtown Employment Survey Report*. City of Miami: Miami. 1983.

Clark, John, and Richard Sykes. Some Determinants of Police Organization and Practice in a Modern Industrial Bureaucracy. In D. Glaser (ed.) *Handbook of Criminology*. Chicago: Rand McNally. 1974.

Clark, John, and Eugene Wenninger. Socio-economic Class and Area Correlates of Illegal Behavior among Juveniles. *American Sociological Review* 27 (1962): 826–834.

Cohen, Lawrence, and Kenneth Land. Discrepancies Between Crime Reports and Crime Surveys: Urban and Structural Determinants. *Criminology* 22 (1984): 499–530.

Cooley, Charles H. *Social Organization*. New York: Scribner. 1909.

Cordner, Gary. A Problem-Oriented Approach to Community-oriented Policing. Paper presented at the first annual Temple University Criminal Justice Symposium. Philadelphia. 1987.

Cox, Steven, and Jack Fitzgerald. *Police in Community Relations*. Dubuque: W. C. Brown Co. 1983.

Crawford, Thomas J. Police Overperception of Ghetto Hostility. *Journal of Police Science and Administration* 1, no. 2 (June 1973): 168–174.

Cumming, Elaine, Ian Cumming, and Laura Edell. Policeman as Philosopher, Guide and Friend. *Social Problems* 12 (1965): 276–286.

Dade County Grand Jury. *Final Report: Police Use of Deadly Force*. Fall 1982. Miami: Dade County. 1983.

———. *Final Report: Immigration and Narcotics Interdiction*. Miami: Dade County. 1982.

Dade-Miami Criminal Justice Council. *Criminal Justice in Dade County*. Miami, 1981.

Davis, Kenneth Culp. *Police Discretion*. St. Paul: West Publishing Co., 1975.

Decker, Scott. Citizens Attitudes Toward the Police. *Journal of Police Science and Administration* 9, no. 1 (March 1981): 80–87.

Department of Human Resources. *Dade County Characteristics*. Miami: Metropolitan Dade County. 1983.

Dukes, Richard, and Geoffrey Alpert. Criminal Victimization from a Police Perspective. *Journal of Police Science and Administration* 8 (1980): 21–30.

Dunham, Roger, and Geoffrey Alpert. Neighborhood Differences in Attitudes Toward Policing. *Journal of Criminal Law and Criminology* 79 (1988).

Erbe, Brigette. Race and Socioeconomic Segregation. *American Sociological Review* 40 (1975): 801–812.

Erez, Edna. Self-Defined "Desert" and Citizens' Assessment of the Police. *Journal of Criminal Law and Criminology* 75 (1984): 1276–1299.

Farr, James, and Frank Landy. The Development and Use of Supervisory and Peer Scales for Police Performance Appraisal. In C. Spielberger (ed.) *Police Selection and Evaluation*. New York: Praeger. 1979. Pp. 61–75.

Flanagan, Timothy. Consumer Perspectives on Police Operational Strategy. *Journal of Police Science and Administration* 13, no. 1 (March 1985): 10–21.

Fogelson, Robert. *Big City Police*. Cambridge: Harvard University Press. 1977.

Fried, Mark, and Peggy Gleicher. Some Sources of Residential Satisfaction in an Urban Slum. *Journal of the American Institute of Planners* 27 (1961): 305–315.

Froemel, Ernest. Objective and Subjective Measures of Police Officer Performance. In C. Spielberger (ed.) *Police Selection and Evaluation*. New York: Praeger. 1979. Pp. 87-111.

Furstenberg, Frank, and Charles Wellford. Calling the Police: The Evaluation of Police Service. *Law and Society Review* 7 (1973): 393–406.

Gabor, Ivan, and Christopher Low. The Police Role in the Community. *Criminology* 10, no. 4 (February 1973): 383–414.

Gaines, Larry, N. Van Tubergen, and M. Paiva. Police Officer Perception of Promotion as a Source of Motivation. *Journal of Criminal Justice* 12, no. 3 (September 1984): 265–275.

Gaiter, Dorothy. No Individual Can Speak for All Blacks. *Miami Herald*. March 27, 1985, p. 27-A.

Gans, Herbert. *The Urban Villagers*. New York: The Free Press. 1962.

Garofalo, James. *Public Opinion About Crime*. Washington, D.C.: U.S. Government Printing Office. 1977.

Geller, William (ed.) *Police Leadership in America: Crisis and Opportunity*. Chicago: American Bar Foundation. 1985.

Gershman, Carl. A Matter of Class. *New York Times Magazine*. October 5, 1980.

Goldstein, Herman. Toward Community-Oriented Policing: Potential, Basic Requirements, and Threshold Questions. *Crime and Delinquency* 33 (January, 1987): 6–30.

———. *Policing in a Free Society*. Cambridge: Ballinger. 1977.

Greenberg, Stephanie, and William Rohe. Informal Social Control and Crime Prevention in Modern Neighborhoods. Pp. 79-118 in R. Taylor (ed.) *Urban Neighborhoods: Research and Policy*. New York: Praeger. 1986.

Greene, Jack, Foot Patrol and Community Policing: Past Practices and Future Prospects. *American Journal of Police* 4 (1987): 1–16.

Greene, Jack, and Ralph Taylor. Community-based Policing and Foot Patrol: Issues of Theory and Evaluation. Paper presented at the First Annual Temple University Criminal Justice Symposium. Philadelphia. 1987.

Greer, Scott. *The Emerging City: Myth and Reality*. New York: The Free Press, 1962.

Groves, Eugene, and Peter Rossi. Police Perceptions of a Hostile Ghetto: Realism or Projection. *American Behavioral Scientist* 13 (May-August 1970): 727–743.

Jacob, Herbert. Black and White Perceptions of Justice in the City. *Law and Society Review* 5 (1978) 69–89.

Janowitz, Morris. *The Community Press in an Urban Setting*. Chicago: University of Chicago Press. 1967.

Janowitz, Morris, and G. Suttles. The Social Ecology of Citizenship. In Rosemary Sarri and Yeheskel Hasenfeld (eds.) *The Management of Human Services*. New York: Columbia University Press. 1978. Pp. 94–112.

Johnson, David. *American Law Enforcement: A History*. St. Louis: Forum Press. 1981.

Hagan, John, A. R. Gillis, and Janet Chan. Explaining Official Delinquency: A Spacial Study of Class, Conflict and Control. *Sociological Quarterly* 19 (1978) 386–398.

Keller, Suzanne. *The Urban Neighborhood: A Sociological Perspective*. New York: Random House. 1968.

Kelling, George. Order Maintenance, the Quality of Urban Life, and Police: A Different Line of Argument. In William Geller (ed.) *Police Leadership in America: Crisis and Opportunity*. New York: Praeger. 1985. Pp. 296–308.

Klockars, Carl. *The Idea of Police*. Beverly Hills: Sage Publications. 1985.

Koverman, Robert. Team Policing: An Alternative to Traditional Law Enforcement Techniques. *Journal of Police Science* 2 (1974): 15–19.

Lander, Bernard. *Towards an Understanding of Juvenile Delinquency*. New York: Columbia University Press. 1954.

Landy, Frank. *Performance Appraisal in Police Departments*. Washington, D.C.: Police Foundation, 1977.

Lefkowitz, Joel. Psychological Attributes of Policemen. *Journal of Social Issues* 31 (1975): 3–26.

Lichter, Linda. Who Speaks for Black America. *Public Opinion* 8, no. 4 (August-September 1985): 41–44, 58.

Lipset, Seymour M., and William Schneider. *The Confidence Gap*. New York: Rinehart and Winston. 1980.

Lipset, Seymour M., and William Schneider. *The Confidence Gap: Business, Labor and Government in the Public Mind*. New York: The Free Press. 1983.

McIver, John, and Roger Parks. Evaluating Police Performance: Identification of Effective and Ineffective Police Actions. In R. Bennett (ed.) *Police At Work: Issues and Analysis*. Beverly Hills: Sage Publicationns. 1983. Pp. 21–44.

Mandel, Michael J. Local Roles and Social Networks. *American Sociological Review* 48 (1983): 376–386.

Manning, Peter. Community Policing. *American Journal of Police* 3 (1984): 205–227.

Mastrofski, Stephan. Police Knowledge: The Impact of Patrol Assignment Patterns on Officer Behavior in Urban Residential Neighborhoods. Ph.D. Dissertation. University of North Carolina, Chapel Hill. 1981.

———. Police Knowledge on the Patrol Beat: A Performance Measure. In R. Bennett (ed.) *Police At Work: Issues and Analysis*. Beverly Hills: Sage Publications. 1983. Pp. 45–64.

——. Dilemmas of Reform: Some Difficult Problems for Community Policing. Paper presented at the Temple University Criminal Justice Symposium. Philadelphia. May 1987.

Meagher, Steven. Police Patrol Styles: How Pervasive is Community Variation? *Journal of Police Science and Administration* 13 (1985): 36–45.

Merry, Sally E. *Urban Danger: Life in a Neighborhood of Strangers.* Philadelphia: Temple University Press. 1981.

Messner, Steven. Inequality and the Homicide Rate. *Criminology* 20 (1982): 103–114.

Miller, Wilbur. *Cops and Bobbies: Police Authority in New York and London 1830–1870.* Chicago: University of Chicago Press. 1977.

Mladenka, Kenneth, and Kim Q. Hill. The Distribution of Urban Police Services. *Journal of Politics* 40 (February 1978): 112–133.

Moore, Mark, and George Kelling. To Serve and Protect: Learning from Police History. *The Public Interest* 70 (1983): 49–65.

Morkkonen, Erik. *Police in Urban America 1860–1920.* Cambridge: Cambridge University Press. 1981.

Morris, David, and Karl Hess. *Neighborhood Power: The New Localism.* Boston: Beacon Press. 1975.

Morstain, Barry. Minority-White Differences on a Police Aptitude Exam. *Psychological Reports* 55 (1984): 515–525.

Muir, William. *Police: Street Corner Politicians.* Chicago: University of Chicago Press. 1977.

Myren, Richard. Decentralization and Citizen Participation in Criminal Justice Systems. *Public Administration Review* 32 (1972): 718–738.

National Advisory Commission on Civil Disorders Report. New York: Bantam Books. 1968.

National Advisory Commission on Criminal Justice Standards and Goals. *Police.* Washington, D.C.: U.S. Government Printing Office. 1973.

National Institute of Justice. *Arrest Convictability as a Measure of Police Performance* (NCJ 80954). Washington, D.C.: U.S. Government Printing Office. 1985.

Nisbet, Robert. Moral Values and Community. *International Review of Community Development* 5 (1960) 79–89.

O'Brien, John. Public Attitudes Toward Police. *Journal of Police Science and Administration* 6 (1978): 303–310.

——. *Crime and Victimization Data.* Beverly Hills: Sage Publications. 1985.

Olson, Bruce. An Exploratory Study of Task Preferences. *Personnel Journal* 49 (1970): 1015–1020.

Olson, Philip. Urban Neighborhood Research: Its Development and Current Focus. *Urban Affairs Quarterly* 17 (1982): 491–518.

Osgood, Charles, George Suci, and Percy Tannenbaum. *The Measurement of Meaning*. Urbana: University of Illinois Press. 1957.

Overtown Blue Ribbon Committee. *Final Report*. Miami: City of Miami. 1984.

Park, Robert. The City: Suggestions for the Investigation of Human Behavior. *American Journal of Sociology* 20 (1915): 577–611.

Park, Robert, Ernest Burgess, and Brodrick McKenzie. *The City*. Chicago: University of Chicago Press. 1925.

Petersen, David. Informal Norms and Police Practice: The Traffic Quota System. *Sociology and Social Research* 55 (1971): 354–362.

———. Police Disposition of the Petty Offender. *Sociology and Social Research*. (April 1972): 320–370.

Police Foundation. *The Newark Foot Patrol Experiment*. Washington, D.C.: The Police Foundation. 1981.

Polk, Kenneth. Juvenile Delinquency and Social Areas. *Social Problems* 5 (1957): 214–317.

Poplin, Dennis. *Communities: A Survey of Theories and Methods of Research*. New York: Macmillan. 1979.

Porter, Bruce, and Marvin Dunn. *The Miami Riot of 1980*. Lexington: Lexington Books. 1984.

President's Commission on Law Enforcement and the Administration of Justice. *The Challenge of Crime in a Free Society*. Washington, D.C.: U.S. Government Printing Office. 1967.

Pugh, George. The Good Police Officer: Qualities, Roles, and Concepts. *Journal of Police Science and Administration* 14 (1986): 1–5.

Reiff, David. A Second Havana. *The New Yorker*. May 15, 1987, pp. 65–87.

Reiss, Albert. *Police and the Public*. New Haven: Yale University Press. 1971.

———. *Policing a City's Central District: The Oakland Story*. Washington, D.C.: U.S. Government Printing Office. 1985.

Reiss, Albert, and David J. Bordua. Environmental and Organization: A Perspective on Police. In D. Bordua (ed.) *The Police: Six Sociological Essays*. New York: Wiley. 1967. Pp. 25–55.

Rousey, Dennis. Cops and Guns: Police Use of Deadly Force in Nineteenth Century New Orleans. *The American Journal of Legal History* 28, no. 1 (January 1984): 41–66.

Rubenstein, Jonathan. *City Police*. New York: Ballantine Books. 1973.

Rumbaut, Ruben, and Egon Bittner. Changing Conceptions of the Police Role: A Sociological Review. In N. Morris and M. Tonry (eds.) *Crime and Justice* (Vol. 1). Chicago: University of Chicago Press. 1979. Pp. 239–288.

Sampson, Robert. Neighborhood and Crime: The Structural Determinants of Personal Victimization. *Journal of Research in Crime and Delinquency* 22 (1985): 7–40.

Sampson, Robert, Thomas Castellano, and John Laub. Analysis of National Crime Survey Data to Study Serious Delinquent Behavior. *Juvenile Criminal Behavior and its Relation to Neighborhood Characteristics.* Washington, D.C.: U.S. Government Printing Office. 1981.

Sandoval, Mercedes. *Mariel and Cuban National Identity.* Miami: Editorial SIBI. 1986.

Scaglion, Richard, and Richard Condon. Determinants of Attitudes Toward City Police. *Criminology* 17 (1980): 485–494.

———. The Structure of Black and White Attitudes Toward Police. *Human Organization* 39 (1980a): 280–283.

Schuman, Howard, and Bary Gruenberg. Dissatisfaction with City Services: Is Race an Important Factor? In Harlan Huhn (ed.) *People and Politics in Urban Society.* Beverly Hills: Sage Publications. 1972. Pp. 369–392.

Sharp, Elaine. Police Performance Measurement: Reactions and a Further Suggestion. *Urban Interest* 4 (1982): 34–40.

Shaw, Clifford, and Henry McKay. *Juvenile Delinquency in Urban Areas.* Chicago: University of Chicago Press. 1942.

———. *Juvenile Delinquency in Urban Areas.* 2nd ed. Chicago: University of Chicago Press. 1969.

Sherman, Lawrence. Policing Communities: What Works? In Alpert Reiss and Michael Tonry (eds.) *Communities and Crime.* Chicago: University of Chicago Press. 1986. Pp. 343–386.

Short, James. Introduction to the Revised Edition. In Clifford Shaw and Henry McKay. *Juvenile Delinquency in Urban Areas.* 2nd ed. Chicago: University of Chicago Press. 1969. Pp. xxv–liv.

Simcha-Fagan, Ora, and Joseph Schwartz. Neighborhood and Delinquency: An Assessment of Contextual Effects. *Criminology* 24 (1986): 667–703.

Skolnick, Jerome, and David Bayley. *The New Blue Line.* N.Y.: Free Press. 1986.

Slovak, Jeffrey. *Styles of Urban Policing.* N.Y.: New York University Press. 1986.

Smith, Douglas. The Neighborhood Context of Police Behavior. In Albert Reiss and Michael Tonry (eds.) *Communities and Crime.* Chicago: University of Chicago Press. 1986. Pp. 313–341.

Smith, Douglas, and Christie Visher. Street-Level Justice: Situational Determinants of Police Arrest Decisions. *Social Problems* 29 (1981): 167–177.

Smith, Paul, and R. Hawkins. Victimization, Types of Citizen-Police Contacts and Attitudes Toward the Police. *Law and Society Review* 8 (1973): 135–152.

Smith, Robert. Measuring Neighborhood Cohesion: A Review and Some Suggestions. *Human Ecology* 3 (1975): 143–160.

Spielberger, Charles (ed.) *Police Selection and Evaluation*. New York: Praeger. 1979.

Spielberger, Charles, John Ward, and Harry Spaulding. A Model for the Selection of Law Enforcement Officers. In C. Spielberger (ed.) *Police Selection and Evaluation*. New York: Praeger. 1979. Pp. 11–29.

Stark, Rodney. *Police Riots*. Belmont, Calif.: Wadsworth. 1972.

State of Florida, Division of Economic Development. *Florida County Comparisons-1984*. Tallahassee: State of Florida. 1985.

Stein, Michael A. *The Eclipse of Community: An Interpretation of American Studies*. Princeton: Princeton University Press. 1960.

Steinman, Michael. Officer Orientations toward the Community. *Urban Affairs Quarterly* 21 (1986): 598–606.

Sterling, James. *Changes in Role Concepts of Police Officers*. Gaithersberg: International Association of Chiefs of Police. 1972.

Sullivan, Peggy, Roger Dunham, and Geoffrey Alpert. Attitude Structures of Different Ethnic and Age Groups Concerning Police. *Journal of Criminal Law and Criminology* 78 (1987): 501–521.

Suttles, George. *The Social Construction of Communities*. Chicago: University of Chicago Press. 1972.

Sykes, Gary. Street Justice: A Moral Defense of Order Maintenance Policing. *Justice Quarterly* 3 (1986): 497–512.

Sykes, Richard, and Edward Brent. The Regulation of Interaction by Police. *Criminology* 18 (1980): 182–197.

Sykes, Richard, and John P. Clark. A Theory of Deference Exchange in Police-Civilian Encounters. *American Journal of Sociology* 81 (1975): 584–600.

Tansik, David, and James Elliot. *Managing Police Organizations*. Monterey: Ouxburg Press. 1981.

Taub, Richard, D. Garth Taylor, and Jan Dunham. *Paths of Neighborhood Change*. Chicago: University of Chicago Press. 1984.

Teahan, John. A Longitudinal Study of Attitude Shifts Among Black and White Police Officers. *Journal of Social Issues* 31 (1975): 47–55.

Terry, Clinton. Police Stress. *Journal of Police Science and Administration* 9 (1981): 61–65.

Thomas, Charles, and Jeffrey Hyman. Perceptions of Crime, Fear of Victimization and Public Perceptions of Police Performance. *Journal of Police Science and Administration* 5 (1977): 305–317.

Trojanowicz, Robert, and Joanne Belknap. Community Policing: Training Issues. Paper presented to the annual meetings of the Academy of Criminal Justice Sciences. 1986.

United States Civil Rights Commission. *Who is Guarding the Guardians?* Washington, D.C.: U.S. Government Printing Office. 1981.

United States Civil Rights Commission. *Confronting Racial Isolation in Miami.* Washington, D.C.: U.S. Printing Office. 1982.

U.S. National Commission on Law Observance and Enforcement, Vol. 11. *Lawlessness in Law Enforcement.* Washington, D.C.: U.S. Printing Office. 1971.

Walker, Darlene, et al. Contact and Support: An Empirical Assessment of Public Attitudes toward the Police and the Courts. *North Carolina Law Review* 51 (1972): 43–79.

Walker, Donald. Black Police Values and the Black Community. *Police Studies* 5 (1983): 20–28.

Walker, Donald, and Peter Krateoski. A Cross Cultural Perspective on Police Values and Police-Community Relations. *Criminal Justice Review* 6 (1985): 17–24.

Walker, Samuel. *A Critical History of Police Reform.* Lexington: Lexington Books. 1977.

———. *The Police in America.* New York: McGraw Hill. 1983.

———. Broken Windows and Fractured History: The Use and Misuse of History in Recent Police Patrol Analysis. *Justice Quarterly* 1 (1984): 75–90.

Webber, David I. Order in Diversity: Community Without Propinquity in R. Gutman and D. Popnoe (eds.) *Neighborhood, City and Metropolis: An Integrated Reader in Urban Sociology.* N.Y.: Random House. 1970.

Werthman, Clark, and Irving Piliavin. Gang Members and the Police. In David Bordua (ed.) *The Police Six Sociological Essays.* New York: Wiley. 1967. Pp. 56–98.

Westley, William A. Violence and the Police. *American Journal of Sociology.* 49 (1953): 34–41.

Whitaker, Gordon, Steven Mastrofski, Elinor Ostrom, Roger Parks, and Stephan Percy. *Basic Issues in Police Performance.* Washington, D.C.: U.S. Government Printing Office. 1982.

White, Mervin, and Ben Menke. A Critical Analysis of Surveys on Public Opinions toward Police Agencies. *Journal of Police Science and Administration* 6, no. 2 (June 1978): 204–218.

White, Susan. A Perspective on Police Professionalism. *Law and Society Review* 7 (1972): 61–85.

Whorf, Benjamin. *Language, Thought and Reality*. New York: John Wiley and Sons. 1956.

Whyte, William F. *Street Corner Society*. Chicago: University of Chicago Press. 1943.

Williams, Hubert, and Antony Pate. Returning to First Principles: Reducing the Fear of Crime in Newark. *Crime and Delinquency* 33 (1987): 53–70.

Wilson, James Q. *Varieties of Police Behavior*. Cambridge: Harvard University Press. 1968.

Wilson, James Q., and George Kelling. The Police and Neighborhood Safety. *The Atlantic Monthly*, March 1982, pp. 29–38.

Wintersmith, Robert. *Police and the Black Community*. Lexington: Lexington Books. 1974.

Index

About the Authors

GEOFFREY P. ALPERT is professor in the College of Criminal Justice at the University of South Carolina. His current research projects involve police corruption, police use of deadly force and (with Roger Dunham) pursuit driving. Dr. Alpert has also conducted evaluations of the recruitment, selection and hiring practices of police officers. His interests center on empirically based decision making for law enforcement and the judiciary.

ROGER G. DUNHAM is an associate professor of sociology at the University of Miami. Dr. Dunham has recently completed a three-year study on the prediction of relapse among alcoholics in treatment, a study funded by the National Institute of Alcohol Abuse and Alcoholism. He is also interested in the application of interactional theories of deviance to problems of juveniles.

CPSIA information can be obtained at www.ICGtesting.com
Printed in the USA
LVOW101436140213

320142LV00008B/125/P